THE UPPER ROOM.

WHERE THE WORLD MEETS TO PRAY

Susan Hibbins
UK Editor

INTERDENOMINATIONAL
INTERNATIONAL
INTERRACIAL

33 LANGUAGES
Multiple formats are available in some languages

CW00606524

The Bible Reading Fellowship
15 The Chambers, Vineyard
Abingdon OX14 3FE
brf.org.uk

The Bible Reading Fellowship (BRF) is a Registered Charity (233280)

ISBN 978 0 85746 767 6
All rights reserved

Originally published in the USA by The Upper Room®
US edition © The Upper Room®
This edition © The Bible Reading Fellowship 2018
Cover image © Thinkstock

Acknowledgements

Scripture quotations marked NRSV are taken from The New Revised Standard Version of the Bible, Anglicised Edition, copyright © 1989, 1995 by the Division of Christian Education of the National Council of the Churches of Christ in the USA. Used by permission. All rights reserved.

Scripture quotations marked NIV are taken from The Holy Bible, New International Version (Anglicised edition) copyright © 1979, 1984, 2011 by Biblica. Used by permission of Hodder & Stoughton Publishers, an Hachette UK company. All rights reserved. 'NIV' is a registered trademark of Biblica. UK trademark number 1448790.

Extracts marked KJV are from the Authorised Version of the Bible (The King James Bible), the rights in which are vested in the Crown, are reproduced by permission of the Crown's Patentee, Cambridge University Press.

Extracts from CEB copyright © 2011 by Common English Bible.

Map on page 6 © Thinkstock.

Printed by Gutenberg Press, Tarxien, Malta

How to use *The Upper Room*

The Upper Room is ideal in helping us spend a quiet time with God each day. Each daily entry is based on a passage of scripture, and is followed by a meditation and prayer. Each person who contributes a meditation to the magazine seeks to relate their experience of God in a way that will help those who use *The Upper Room* every day.

Here are some guidelines to help you make best use of *The Upper Room*:

1 Read the passage of scripture. It is a good idea to read it more than once, in order to have a fuller understanding of what it is about and what you can learn from it.
2 Read the meditation. How does it relate to your own experience? Can you identify with what the writer has outlined from their own experience or understanding?
3 Pray the written prayer. Think about how you can use it to relate to people you know, or situations that need your prayers today.
4 Think about the contributor who has written the meditation. Some users of the *The Upper Room* include this person in their prayers for the day.
5 Meditate on the 'Thought for the day' and the 'Prayer focus', perhaps using them again as the focus for prayer or direction for action.

Why is it important to have a daily quiet time? Many people will agree that it is the best way of keeping in touch every day with the God who sustains us, and who sends us out to do his will and show his love to the people we encounter each day. Meeting with God in this way reassures us of his presence with us, helps us to discern his will for us and makes us part of his worldwide family of Christian people through our prayers.

I hope that you will be encouraged as you use the magazine regularly as part of your daily devotions, and that God will richly bless you as you read his word and seek to learn more about him.

Susan Hibbins
UK Editor

CAN YOU HELP?

Here at BRF, we're always looking for ways to promote the practice of daily Bible reading, and we would like to ask for your help in spreading the word about this valuable resource.

Can I ask you to spread the word about the usefulness of *The Upper Room* in aiding daily meditation and prayer? This could be among your friends and contacts, or at any events in which you might be involved, such as church or a Bible study group, or a conference, special service, retreat or workshop.

We would really value your help, and we'll happily send you some sample copies if you can use them. Just let me know how many you would like and I'll arrange for them to be sent to you. If you wish you can email me at **susan.hibbins@brf.org.uk**.

If you're active on social media, we can supply cover graphics for use on Twitter, Facebook and so on, and we can also supply information packs to churches and groups if you pass on any requests to me.

Thank you in advance for helping us to publicise our Bible reading notes.

Susan Hibbins
UK Editor, The Upper Room

Living resolutions

They devoted themselves to the apostles' teaching and to fellowship, to the breaking of bread and to prayer. Everyone was filled with awe at the many wonders and signs performed by the apostles.
Acts 2:42–43 (NIV)

As a new year begins, I hear conversations about resolutions and goals. We make lists on social media of books we plan to read, places we want to travel to and habits we hope to break or take up. Sometimes I wonder if we get too caught up in listing and talking about our hopes and goals. After all, talking about the fresh start offered by our New Year's resolutions is the easy part. Living those resolutions can be much more challenging.

In this issue of *The Upper Room,* many of our writers share stories about the challenge and importance of actions that reflect Christ's grace, love and mercy to the world – serving others without recognition or attending to the small details of daily life. In Acts 2, the early Christian community broke bread together, spent time in fellowship with one another, gave to those in need and praised God. These actions led others to explore the way of Christ and forged the community that became the church.

In my experience, the faithful actions and attitudes of others have helped me to see Christ in the world, inspiring me to live in more Christlike ways. I think of friends and family who have prayed for and supported me in times of grief and joy. I think of mentors who have listened deeply and given me the gift of their presence when I needed guidance.

As you read, reflect and pray, I hope you will consider these questions. Where do you see Christ at work in your life and in your community? How will you live a life that honours Christ this year? I hope that for all of us, 2019 will be a year filled with the joy of serving Christ through serving others.

Lindsay L. Gray
Editorial Director, The Upper Room

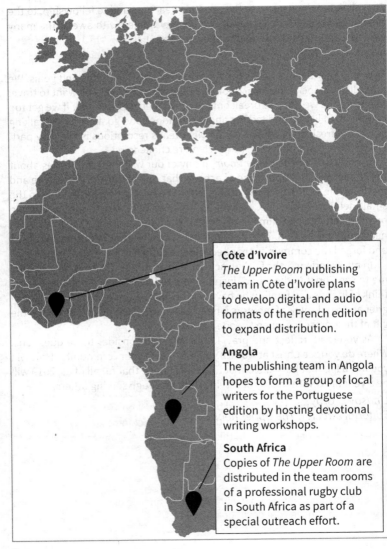

Côte d'Ivoire
The Upper Room publishing team in Côte d'Ivoire plans to develop digital and audio formats of the French edition to expand distribution.

Angola
The publishing team in Angola hopes to form a group of local writers for the Portuguese edition by hosting devotional writing workshops.

South Africa
Copies of *The Upper Room* are distributed in the team rooms of a professional rugby club in South Africa as part of a special outreach effort.

The Editor writes...

In Mark's gospel, we read the short account of Jesus calling his first disciples (Mark 1:16–20). Jesus walks beside the Sea of Galilee, where he sees fishermen Simon and Andrew casting a net into the lake, and he invites them to follow him. A little further on, Jesus sees James and John preparing their nets aboard their boat, and asks the same of them. In each case, the two sets of brothers leave their nets and follow Jesus. James and John also leave their father Zebedee behind in the boat with the other men who work for them.

I wonder what sort of day that was. Was the lakeside noisy, crowded with busy people? Did the sunshine sparkle on the water, so that Jesus had to shade his eyes to see the men clearly? It is interesting to note that all four men leave everything behind 'at once' and 'without delay', presumably with no second thoughts. Had they seen Jesus before this day? Perhaps the four men had listened to Jesus' preaching (see v. 14) and had already warmed to him, so much so that when Jesus invited them to follow him and work with him, they did not hesitate.

For me, the most important detail in these short verses is that Jesus calls the disciples exactly where they are: at work, performing tasks that were part of their daily lives. He did not wait for them to attend the synagogue to see if they were worthy people to join him; he was not interested in their past; he did not look for character references from other people.

How about us? Do we think we need special qualifications before we can be Jesus' disciples: many years' attendance at church, for example, and reading our Bible each day? Jesus might be glad that we do these things, but I think he is more interested in us now, just as we are, with all our strengths and weaknesses. When we have listened to his voice and heard his call, all he wants from us is a positive 'Yes'. Jesus knew the disciples' potential. They were slow to learn, sometimes quarrelsome and prone to letting him down, but Jesus knew what they would become. And he knows the same about us.

The disciples left their nets and former lives behind that day for the biggest adventure of their lives. In this new year, are we ready to do the same?

Susan Hibbins
UK Editor

The Bible readings are selected with great care, and we urge you to include the suggested reading in your devotional time.

New Year's resolution

Read Psalm 67:1–7

Truly my soul finds rest in God; my salvation comes from him.
Psalm 62:1 (NIV)

It was New Year's Eve and, while everyone else was busy preparing for the evening's events, I spent some time thinking about what my New Year's resolution would be. Then it occurred to me that my family could probably suggest some good resolutions. After all, they know me better than anyone.

Later I carefully considered all their suggestions and decided on just being me. They had probably suggested this because I often worry about everyone else so much that I get lost in their problems, which leaves me no time to just be me. That night as I was getting ready for bed, I was thinking about what I could do to make this resolution work. Then it hit me: I didn't have to plan! All I needed was my salvation, my family and my God.

Prayer: *Heavenly Father, be with us all year long. Help us to focus on you in all that we do, and help us to trust that you are right by our side every day. In Jesus' name, we pray. Amen*

Thought for the day: How do I want the Lord to help me be me in the coming year?

Bristol E. DeSpain (Missouri)

'Where is the new?'

Read 2 Corinthians 5:16–21

Whatever is true, whatever is honourable, whatever is just, whatever is pure, whatever is pleasing, whatever is commendable… think about these things.
Philippians 4:8 (NRSV)

It was 31 December, and three-year-old Julu was excited and happy, playing and singing repeatedly, 'Tomorrow is the New Year. Everything will be new tomorrow!' After supper, with much expectation, Julu went off to sleep.

Early the next morning Julu got up, ran outside, and then came back to the sitting room. In a loud disappointed voice, he asked, 'Where is the new? Nothing is new outside; there is nothing new inside. Where is the New Year?'

Then I wondered if sometimes I can't see the newness in my life. Suddenly Bible verses about newness came to mind. From 2 Corinthians 5:17, I remembered, 'If anyone is in Christ, the new creation has come' (NIV). I asked myself, 'Am I in Christ today? What are the signs that I am a new creation?' Philippians 4:8 gives a clue. Whatever is true, noble, right, pure, lovely, admirable and praiseworthy is what I am to think constantly about. A second clue comes from Galatians 5:22–23. If I am a new creation, the fruit of the Spirit – 'love, joy, peace, forbearance, kindness, goodness, faithfulness, gentleness and self-control' – will be evident in my life. Thank God for the chance to become a new creation in Christ!

Prayer: *Dear God, give us wisdom to guide us in our life's journey, and lead us to life eternal. In Jesus' name. Amen*

Thought for the day: How am I leading a Christ-centred life?

Sriparna Mahanty (Odisha, India)

God's tree climbers

Read Luke 19:1–10

[Jesus] said to him, 'Zacchaeus, hurry and come down; for I must stay at your house today.'
Luke 19:5 (NRSV)

Zacchaeus was a wealthy tax collector, who also happened to be short in stature. His wealth could buy him access to many things, but a front-row seat to see Jesus wasn't one of them. Instead, Zacchaeus had to resort to climbing a tree in order to catch a glimpse of Jesus.

To me, even the thought of clambering up a tree is more than a little scary. Yet Zacchaeus was willing to risk perhaps a futile climb and personal embarrassment for the chance to see Jesus.

Jesus asks us to come to him with the innocence of a child (see Matthew 18:3). No wonder that when he saw Zacchaeus in a tree, he immediately offered to pay him a visit. As a result, Zacchaeus' life was changed: he gave to the poor, made restitution to those he had cheated and, most importantly, received salvation.

Jesus came to seek and save the lost – and whether we are up a tree or lost in the woods, I take comfort in the fact that Jesus longs to rescue us. Whenever I feel unsure or embarrassed about the next step God is calling me to take, I remember Zacchaeus. If he was willing to take a risk just to see Jesus, how much more should I be willing to risk following the Master?

Prayer: *Father God, grant us the courage and humility to seek your Son, even when it seems risky to do so. In Jesus' name. Amen*

Thought for the day: It's risky to walk with Jesus, but the rewards are eternal.

Phillip Catterton (Kansas, US)

Comfort after loss

Read Jeremiah 31:12–14

Blessed are those who mourn, for they will be comforted.
Matthew 5:4 (NIV)

I always assumed that I would have children. A year after my husband and I married, we were ecstatic to learn that we were expecting our first child. But two weeks later, we lost the child to an early miscarriage, and we were left reeling in grief. It was incredible how attached we had already grown in just 13 short days to that tiny life growing inside me. Gleefully, we'd shared our news with many friends and family members, unable to hold back our excitement. Now, we had to mourn the child we would never get the chance to know.

I cried many tears over that lost baby, and over every dream we lost along with it – the dream of holding our baby, of hearing his or her first word, of seeing our child grow and develop a unique personality. Having no idea whether a healthy pregnancy would be part of our future was distressing and frightening. Would we ever become parents?

Even in our grief and suffering, however, we were blessed. Our church community, family and friends surrounded us with love and compassion, listening to us and comforting us as we grieved. Through our shared grief, my husband and I came to understand and trust one another and God more deeply. In Christ, we found strength to move forward. Eventually, we were able to have two healthy children; but God's presence during that time of grief assured us that no matter what had happened, he would still have been good.

Prayer: *Dear God, thank you for comforting us when we mourn. Remind us that mourning is a blessing, for it draws us closer to you. Amen*

Thought for the day: Mourning leads me to seek God's comfort.

Kate Underwood (Kentucky, US)

Good-news carriers

Read Romans 10:12–18

How can they hear without someone preaching to them? And how can anyone preach unless they are sent? As it is written: 'How beautiful are the feet of those who bring good news!'

Romans 10:14–15 (NIV)

When I was young, I had a paper round. Every morning, like clockwork, my trusty black-and-white bicycle and I could be found on the streets of my route. I kept going through all kinds of weather so that my customers could read in detail about the events happening around the world. I felt privileged that so many trusted me to provide this benefit to their lives, and I took the responsibility seriously.

The apostles were called to spread much greater news of their time, the news of Jesus – his life and message. Travelling the countryside, they spread the good news of God's love and spoke of the sacrifice of Jesus Christ, which meant that the people's sins could be forgiven. And what a message! Jesus was sent to earth for all men and women of all races, whether rich or poor, powerful or not so powerful. Jesus is Lord, the Son of God.

The apostles faced many obstacles beyond extremes of weather. Rejection, prison and even death stood in the path of these carriers of the gospel, yet they persevered. We too can follow the apostles' example and find opportunities each day to spread the good news.

Prayer: *Dear Lord, may we always be ready to share your word when we have the opportunity. Amen*

Thought for the day: Every day, I will look for opportunities to share the gospel.

Michael J.M. Hotchkiss (Texas, US)

God of restoration

Read Philippians 4:10–13

The Lord restored the fortunes of Job when he had prayed for his friends; and the Lord gave Job twice as much as he had before.
Job 42:10 (NRSV)

In January 1995, our family went through a very difficult time. While we were away on holiday, an early morning knock at the door brought the news that our car had been vandalised and our house burned almost entirely to the ground. What we had in our suitcases and what we were wearing were now all that we owned.

Throughout this crisis, God's helping hand was immediate. We were able to stay in the church manse which was vacant at the time. It was a comfortable accommodation and was offered free of charge for six months. Then a Christian friend organised a fundraiser for us, which we accepted with gratitude. Another friend gave us a Bible, which I still cherish. While we lost many precious items, our lives were safe – and we experienced love that we will never forget.

We now live on two and a half acres of land in the country; God's blessings have continued daily and we have learned that no loss is too big for him to restore.

Prayer: *We thank you, God, for always watching over us – especially in our struggles. Amen*

Thought for the day: I am assured of God's love, even in the most difficult circumstances.

Margaret Young (New South Wales, Australia)

'See, I am doing a new thing!'

Read Isaiah 43:18–21

Forget the former things; do not dwell on the past.
Isaiah 43:18 (NIV)

Each New Year is another chance to achieve what we have not yet achieved. This year I want to be a hard-working student and athlete. However, I sometimes worry that my past failures will affect my future. In 2 Corinthians 5, we read that God does not count our failures and sins against us as long as we are living in Christ. Being afraid that we cannot accomplish our dreams because of our past affects our successes in the future.

Scripture tells us not to worry; we are a new creation. Relying on God's word, I try to keep on track with my studies through continual review and listening closely to my teachers' directions. In the same way, I keep up with my running through practice and mental discipline.

I cannot realise these goals, however, apart from my focus on God. Doing what God wants is our main focus; our love for him motivates us to work hard to achieve our goals. Our purpose in everything we do is to glorify God. As we move into the future, we can rely on him no matter what happens in any New Year.

Prayer: *God of new beginnings, be with us during this New Year. Help us not to dwell on our past failures, but instead to enjoy new days in your presence. Amen*

Thought for the day: I will not let the past take my focus away from God's purpose for me.

Robert Ganzert (North Carolina, US)

The promise of forgiveness

Read Matthew 6:9–15

If you forgive other people when they sin against you, your heavenly Father will also forgive you.
Matthew 6:14 (NIV)

Years ago I found myself sitting on the front steps of my house, listening while the person sitting beside me was breaking my heart. In tears and anger, I pushed the hurt deep down inside and thought, 'I'll get back at him one day.' I wish I had said, 'I forgive you.' It took me a long time to learn that holding on to anger and refusing to forgive someone doesn't take the pain away. It only makes it linger.

Scripture reminds us that in order to be forgiven, we must forgive. I don't know anyone who doesn't want or need forgiveness from time to time. Yet sometimes we hold on to bitterness and lose the very thing that could set us free – the act of forgiving.

Choosing to forgive doesn't mean that the other person gets off without any consequences. It means that we give up our right to take matters into our own hands and instead trust God to do what only he can do. If we ask with a repentant heart, God is willing to forgive. As children of God, we can choose to be just as willing to forgive others.

Prayer: *Dear Lord, help us to forgive those who have wronged us, just as you forgive us. Amen*

Thought for the day: In gratitude for God's forgiveness, I will forgive others.

Christine Baker (Louisiana, US)

Look around

Read Jeremiah 2:4–8

The Lord says: What wrong did your ancestors find in me that made them wander so far? They pursued what was worthless and became worthless.

Jeremiah 2:5 (CEB)

I have a double pushchair for my twin daughters. Its rigid canopy normally stays over their heads like an umbrella, but it can be pulled down so that it covers their faces. The last time we took them to the zoo, for some reason known only to four-year-olds, they were determined to keep the canopy pulled down across their eyes for the entire visit. I would pull up the canopy and proclaim with great enthusiasm, 'Look at the size of those giraffes!' But then, four little hands would immediately reach up and pull the canopy back down. Amazing sights were all around them, but they missed everything. It was a frustrating three hours.

But who am I to complain? How many times has God said, 'Look at the comfort of my promises,' but I refuse to look by not studying the Bible? God says, 'Talk to me; I have so much to give you,' but I daydream instead. God tells me, 'You can do things that will not only bless you now but will store up treasures in heaven,' but I go and waste my time doing other things. How many times have I reached up and pulled the blinkers back down over my eyes?

God has surrounded us with many assurances and blessings. If we will only reach out in faith and grab hold of them, then we will be able to proclaim, 'Look at the size of those blessings!'

Prayer: *Dear Lord, may our eyes always be open to your abundant blessings. Amen*

Thought for the day: Every day, I will look around to see God's great blessings.

Bob LaForge (New Jersey, US)

Restore with love

Read Colossians 3:12–14

Be completely humble and gentle; be patient, bearing with one another in love.
Ephesians 4:2 (NIV)

I recently read an article about a tribe in northern Natal in South Africa. According to tribal custom, when someone does something wrong or detrimental to others, the members of the tribe take the offender to the centre of the village and surround him or her. Over two days, the tribe members tell the offender the good things he or she has accomplished. The purpose of the ritual is to restore the person and to affirm that he or she is essentially a good person.

I think that too often our tendency is to treat others unkindly, especially when they have made a mistake. We make sure to remind them continuously of their errors. Even in raising our children, we tend to emphasise the negative rather than the positive.

However, the Bible teaches love. In Matthew 22:39, Jesus says, 'Love your neighbour as yourself.' Galatians 6:1 reminds us, 'If someone is caught in a sin, you who live by the Spirit should restore that person gently.' Let us treat others the way we want to be treated. In doing so, we'll follow the example of Jesus, who loves us, even though we do not merit it.

Prayer: *Loving God, we confess that we are not perfect. Forgive us and teach us to follow your example of mercy. Amen*

Thought for the day: Surrounding people with love can bring healing and restore the community.

Narda Vargas (Dominican Republic)

The aroma of Christ

Read 2 Corinthians 2:14–17

Thanks be to God, who in Christ always leads us in triumphal procession, and through us spreads in every place the fragrance that comes from knowing him.
2 Corinthians 2:14 (NRSV)

Walking on our northern Utah hiking paths gives me a great appreciation of God's majesty. My eyes delight in the beauty of snow-covered Wasatch peaks and the sunlight sparkling on the Great Salt Lake. My senses awaken to the lowing of the cows and the chatter of the magpies. As the brisk breeze sweeps over my face, my soul cannot help but praise the Maker of it all.

As beautiful as these surroundings are, along my favourite path the odour of skunk – rank, strong and often lasting for days – is common. As I passed through a 'skunky patch' recently, I wondered about the fragrance that I leave behind in my daily interactions with others. Paul reminded us that we are 'the aroma of Christ' and through us God spreads this fragrance everywhere.

As my nose winced at the smell of the skunk, I had to wonder about times when my 'fragrance' has been more of a stench – times when I might have hung on to anger and bitterness or wallowed in self-centredness. Have I caused others to turn up their noses at Christianity because of my spiritual stink? That is not the witness I desire! But as I spend time seeking God's presence in the Bible and in prayer, his power purifies me. The fragrance I share with the world then becomes the aroma of Christ's love, grace and truth.

Prayer: *Dear Jesus, thank you for transforming us – equipping us to carry your fragrance of life and love to the world. Amen*

Thought for the day: Every day I will seek to spread the fragrance of Christ.

Andrea Nelson (Utah, US)

Answering our cries

Read Matthew 7:7–11

The Lord's eyes watch the righteous, his ears listen to their cries for help.
Psalm 34:15 (CEB)

During the week, my wife cares for two of our grandsons. At two years old, the younger one, Colton, still struggles with his vocabulary so that even when he can find a word to use, he also cries out. He especially loves his toy trains and cries if he can't find them. Whatever the cry, we respond because we love him.

In that respect, God is no different. He watches over us and answers our cries for help. He can hear my cries along with millions of others at the same time. Some days, Colton is needier than usual and wears out his grandmother. But God is more powerful than my wife. Our cries for help never wear him out.

Some of my cries may be insignificant, but God doesn't restrict our access to times of utter crisis or emergency. We are invited to come to him at any time, as a little child would, and that's what I do. As the parent, God listens to our small concerns and complex issues alike. His answers to my cries are always in my best interest, whether I think so or not. Like any good parent, he loves to give good gifts to us.

Prayer: *Dear Father, thank you for hearing and answering our cries for help. Amen*

Thought for the day: Whatever my need, God hears my cries.

Martin Wiles (South Carolina, US)

Welcoming all

Read James 2:1–9

[The Lord declares,] 'I will show my love to the one I called "Not my loved one". I will say to those called "Not my people", "You are my people"; and they will say, "You are my God."'
Hosea 2:23 (NIV)

At each Sunday service, a man at my church sits in the last pew and greets everyone who enters. It doesn't matter who wanders into the church: stranger, newcomer or homeless person. If he doesn't know the visitor, he introduces himself and asks for his or her name. At the sharing of the peace, he walks down to where that new person sits and shakes his or her hand.

I love this man's spirit. It is the spirit of Jesus, for Jesus stands ready to welcome each and every one of us regardless of our circumstances. Our Lord calls us by name and takes our hand. Jesus loved and welcomed all to his teachings and promise of life eternal. I pray that I may always follow this example – not only on Sunday but on each day of the week.

Prayer: *Gracious God, thank you for sending your Son, Jesus Christ, to show us the way to live. Help us always to follow his example and show kindness to everyone. Amen*

Thought for the day: God loves me and knows me by name.

Monica A. Andermann (New York, US)

In the same boat

Read Matthew 8:23–27

[Jesus] replied, 'You of little faith, why are you so afraid?' Then he got up and rebuked the winds and the waves, and it was completely calm.
Matthew 8:26 (NIV)

I had just finished my primary school education and by God's grace I passed my exams and was the best pupil in my area. Everyone was happy for me, and I remember that my friends kept telling me that God was good to me; but I was troubled. My mind was not at peace and sleep eluded me. I was worried that, although I had passed and could now attend a prestigious school to continue my education, my family could not afford to send me. My faith assured me that God, who had been with me this far, would see me through, but my family was in financial crisis.

I thought of the time when Jesus and his disciples were crossing over to the other side of the lake. Even though the disciples knew that Jesus was in the boat with them, they were still troubled. We do the same. Jesus is in the boat with us, but when trouble comes we forget that we can depend on someone greater than the trouble we are going through. In fact, Jesus was asleep because he knew there was no reason to panic. When they woke him, Jesus said, 'You of little faith, why are you so afraid?' Then he rebuked the wind and it was calm.

I eventually received a scholarship that took me through my four years at school. When we remember that Jesus is in the boat with us, we can trust him to calm the storms.

Prayer: *Heavenly Father, help us to remember who you are and that you are with us, even in times of trouble. Amen*

Thought for the day: Today, I will remember that Jesus is in the boat with me.

Mary Nyokabi Penparadise (Kiambu, Kenya)

Purposeful prayer

Read 1 Timothy 2:1–8

If my people, who are called by my name, will humble themselves and pray and seek my face and turn from their wicked ways, then I will hear from heaven, and I will forgive their sin and will heal their land.
2 Chronicles 7:14 (NIV)

Recently, as I stood at the newspaper stand in the supermarket, I found my heart sinking fast at the headlines I was reading: political concerns for our country's future; activities and threats of terrorists; and on a more local level, the issues of drug dependence and alcohol abuse. With a heavy heart, I headed for home, pondering whether there was anything I could honestly do about any of these varied situations.

Later, as I was seeking help and a more positive outlook, I came across two passages of scripture that brought not only hope but also a practical way forward. In 1 Timothy 2, we are called to prayer, not as a last resort but as our first priority, praying for everyone and especially for those who rule over us. Then, 2 Chronicles 7:14 invites us humbly to seek God, interceding and offering up prayers for the healing and restoration of our nation and its people. Now, instead of wondering whether there is anything I can do to help, I find purpose and direction for my prayers.

Prayer: *Heavenly Father, we pray for the healing and restoration of our nation and its people. Amen*

Thought for the day: We are called to prayerful action, not despair.

Mandy Slade (Somerset, England)

Busy days

Read Colossians 2:6–10

Just as you received Christ Jesus as Lord, continue to live your lives in him, rooted and built up in him, strengthened in the faith as you were taught, and overflowing with thankfulness.
Colossians 2:6–7 (NIV)

One day at school, I had two tests, neither of which I had studied for. A friend was having a really bad morning, and she also had a test that day. I felt bad for her, but I told myself there was nothing I could do. I had to study for my tests later in the day; I needed to get good grades. Later in the day, I realised that dismissing my friend had been wrong. Good grades are important, but so is being a good friend – especially when someone is having a tough day.

Often the busyness of everyday life makes it a challenge to live up to our Christian values and we forget to walk in the steps of Jesus. Life is not just about school work, material possessions or all the activities that bring us pleasure. Life is also about doing good for others and shining the light of Christ into the lives of people around us.

By walking in Jesus' footsteps we can help our world to become kinder and more compassionate. No matter how busy our lives may be, as Christians our true mission is to notice those in dark places and to shine the light of God's love on them.

Prayer: *Dear God, help us not to be consumed by busy lives and always to find time to share your love with others. In Jesus' name. Amen*

Thought for the day: In the midst of a busy world, I will walk in the footsteps of Jesus.

Jenny Iruela (North Carolina, US)

House of God

Read Ephesians 2:11–22

In [Christ] the whole building is joined together and rises to become a holy temple in the Lord. And in him you too are being built together to become a dwelling in which God lives by his Spirit.
Ephesians 2:21–22 (NIV)

I was standing near a large building that was about to be demolished. It had once provided office space for many businesses and organisations, and my church used to rent a worship area in it. While standing there, I thought about the day I first attended a Sunday service in that building. I received a warm welcome and found my spiritual home – a life-changing experience for me.

I learned to know Jesus and God's word. I met many wonderful people who became my brothers and sisters in faith. They are faithful and trustworthy friends, who are always there when I need them. My heart is filled with gratitude for these people and the building where I first encountered them.

That old building was demolished to make way for a supermarket. Today we worship in premises that are owned by our church; they suit our needs well and are located not far from the old building.

Even though I have fond memories of the old place, the apostle Paul's words in Ephesians remind me that the building is not the church; Christians make up the church. Paul writes that together we 'become a holy temple in the Lord'. How wonderful it is when we find our spiritual home among fellow Christians!

Prayer: *Dear God, thank you for the gift of fellowship with other Christians. In Jesus' name, we pray. Amen*

Thought for the day: My church is much more than a building.

Riho Pors (Estonia)

God's assurance

Read Matthew 28:1–10, 16–20

Do not fear, for I am with you; do not be dismayed, for I am your God.
Isaiah 41:10 (NIV)

Lightning zipped across the sky with thunder roaring on its heels, as we drove from downtown Seattle to Duvall, Washington. From the back seat my nine-year-old great-niece cried out in fear. Twisting around, I saw her small body shaking and tears streaming down her cheeks. I felt helpless because I couldn't reach her from the front seat. Suddenly she stopped crying. I turned again and saw my grandson, Palmer, rubbing his cousin's arm softly and saying, 'It's okay, Kayla. Think of something fun. Remember how we beat the other cousins today in a race at the park?' She giggled and nodded. The lightning and thunder increased and lasted for the entire hour's drive, but with no more cries from Kayla because Palmer kept his arms around her, soothing her with his words.

I smiled, proud of Palmer as I remembered how often God calms my fears. As a child of God, I know that in times of crisis or challenge, he encircles me and calms my fears. I remember how he gave reassurance to the Israelites: 'Do not fear, for I am with you.' And Jesus reaffirmed the promise: 'And remember, I am with you always, to the end of the age' (Matthew 28:20, NRSV). Like Kayla, I am calmed by the loving arms of Jesus. And his promise of protection and comfort assures me that everything will work out.

Prayer: *God of all comfort, thank you for your constant presence with us and for your word that assures us of protection and comfort. Amen*

Thought for the day: When fears and doubts arise, I can rely on God's promises.

Arlene Rains Graber (Kansas, US)

God can

Read Acts 3:1–10

[Jesus said,] 'Ask and it will be given to you; seek and you will find; knock and the door will be opened to you.'
Luke 11:9 (NIV)

When my children were young, I would ask them to do something like pick up toys in their rooms or make their beds. Sometimes they responded, 'I'm too little!' even when they were big enough to perform the task. They were just not ready to accept responsibility for having that ability yet.

As children, we might have said, 'I'm too little.' As adults we tend to say, 'I can't.' But sometimes when we say we can't do something, we are closing down all possibilities without even trying. All too often, we say we can't when in fact we should more honestly say that we won't, for a variety of reasons.

When Peter told the lame man to stand up and walk, he didn't respond by saying, 'I can't.' He had faith that the power of God had healed him, and he stood up, walking and leaping and praising God! I don't want to limit the possibilities that God has for me – shutting things down by saying, 'I can't' without even trying. With God, all things are possible (see Matthew 19:26).

Prayer: *Dear Lord, open our eyes to the things that seem impossible to us, but which can happen through you. Amen*

Thought for the day: What is God inviting me to do today, to which I will say 'I can'?

David McCain (Louisiana, US)

One day at a time

Read Luke 12:22–31

[Jesus said,] 'Take my yoke upon you and learn from me, for I am gentle and humble in heart, and you will find rest for your souls.'
Matthew 11:29 (NIV)

Struggling with the grief of widowhood, I've had days where even the touch of my clothes seems uncomfortable, and I wonder how I can carry on by myself. I worry about how long I will be able to maintain my house and survive on my own. When I feel this way, I remember Jesus' words, 'Come to me, all you who are weary and burdened, and I will give you rest' (Matthew 11:28). I remember thinking that I just needed to keep pressing on, listening for God's guidance. It was too easy to get ahead of myself and worry about my future.

After a while I discovered the secret to my getting through. It is just by living – at times minute by minute, hour by hour or day by day. All these days added together are two and a half years; while I still struggle, I know I am stronger and that further healing is coming. I know that if I continue to trust and remain obedient, God will lead me – one day at a time.

Prayer: *Heavenly Father, release us from our worries about the future, and help us to trust you for all our days. Amen*

Thought for the day: God carries us into the future one day at a time.

Lenore Warton (New South Wales, Australia)

Small mercies

Read Lamentations 3:22–23

I will praise you, Lord… for great is your love, reaching to the heavens; your faithfulness reaches to the skies.
Psalm 57:9–10 (NIV)

I am reminded of a saying of my mother's: 'Be thankful for small mercies.'

As a carer, life has its difficulties, and there are many things that cannot be changed. But it is possible to develop an attitude of thankfulness and an awareness of God's small mercies, which are there if we can recognise them among the stresses of daily life. It may be the comforting words of a friend who phones frequently, practical offers of assistance, unexpected kindness shown or something as basic as a good night's sleep.

God's mercies are all around us in nature: the first snowdrops emerging in a gloomy January, primroses on a grassy bank or the wonderful colours of autumn.

We can become stuck on the big problems and be blind to the small encouragements which we may take for granted. Life can be chaotic but there is light in the darkness if we look for it.

God's mercies are endless; they are new every morning.

Prayer: *Dear God, help me to know that your presence is with me at all times, especially when things are difficult. Amen*

Thought for the day: I will appreciate the small mercies I encounter each day.

Anne Rasmussen (Somerset, England)

Adopted

Read Romans 8:12–17

To all who did receive him, to those who believed in his name, he gave the right to become children of God.
John 1:12 (NIV)

My parents took me into their home when I was three months old. After that, every detail of their lives was scrutinised before they could adopt me. Their friends testified as character references. Social workers made many unannounced visits to see what kind of care I was receiving. My parents finally were able to adopt me legally when I was eleven months old.

Knowing all that my parents went through to adopt me helps me appreciate how much they wanted me as part of their family. Children at school would tease me about being adopted, but nothing they said could convince me that I am not special to my parents. I know I am special because my parents chose me to be in their family. They had to prove that they wanted me and would take good care of me.

Every one of us is even more special to God. After all, he became human in Jesus Christ, who died for us so that we could be adopted as God's children. God has chosen us and has called everyone to join his family by trusting in Jesus.

Prayer: *Heavenly Father, thank you for giving us your Son so that we can be adopted into your family. Help us to show our love to you by following you in faith, word and deed. Amen*

Thought for the day: Every person is special to God.

Mary Ann Baker (Pennsylvania, US)

Rich in faith

Read James 1:12–16

Blessed is the one who perseveres under trial because, having stood the test, that person will receive the crown of life that the Lord has promised to those who love him.
James 1:12 (NIV)

With rent, utility bills, medication, food and anything else required for day-to-day living, my wife and I often find ourselves struggling to live on our small, fixed income. We try to plan ahead to buy only what we need – to make a shopping list and stick to it. This way, we know that we will have both enough to live on and enough left for the unexpected. This system works well with one major exception. Sticking to a list is hard when so much outside that list looks so good, things we really want but can't afford. Fighting the temptation to buy on impulse is never easy; it requires discipline.

As Christians, we also try to live our lives with discipline. We read the Bible each day, focus on what we need and give thanks for what we have rather than worrying over what we don't have. Like balancing a monthly budget, practising disciplined faith gets easier. We have learned that it's not what we want that really matters, but what we have. Being rich in faith is priceless.

Prayer: *Dear Lord, help us to avoid the temptations of this world and instead to store up treasure in you. Amen*

Thought for the day: Material things come and go, but spiritual wealth lasts forever.

Mark A. Carter (Oregon, US)

Sustained

Read Psalm 62:5–7

[God says,] 'Cry out to me whenever you are in trouble; I will deliver you.'
Psalm 50:15 (CEB)

'So this time will be your hat trick,' the surgeon said with a grin. His words shocked me, given my medical history. My oncologist had spotted a nodule during my MRI scan and declared that to treat this I had to undergo what would be my third operation in three consecutive years. Sitting in the clinic with my husband and my sister, I could find no words. My voice became weak as if all energy and life had been drained out of me. Gathering myself up, I managed to say, 'Doctor, my son is only five.' Then I started crying helplessly.

A short time later, I was praying and meditating when I heard a voice speaking to me, saying, 'I did not forsake you earlier; I will not forsake you now. I am with you.' My third operation was a success, and the biopsy was all clear. God sustained me through five months of chemotherapy – just as he had sustained me through the three painful operations.

I thanked God for his amazing grace and faithfulness. Having travelled a road of many miracles, I am a true witness to the power of Christ my Lord and my Saviour, with many testimonies to share. Praise be to God!

Prayer: *Thank you, gracious God, for your love and mercy. Help us to trust you, and strengthen us so that we can be your true witnesses. In Jesus' name. Amen*

Thought for the day: God is my shield.

Anoshi Naeem (Punjab, Pakistan)

Lost and found

Read Luke 15:11–24

[The father said to his servants,] 'This son of mine was dead and is alive again; he was lost and is found.' So they began to celebrate.
Luke 15:24 (NIV)

Recently, our cat, Charlie, managed to sneak outside and disappear. For two weeks, our family searched the neighbourhood, prayed and even gave out flyers with her picture on them. But sadly we couldn't find her. As hope began to fade, God answered our prayers and Charlie returned home safe and sound.

This experience reminded me of the parable of the prodigal son. Like the younger son in this parable, I sometimes stray from God's home and choose my own path. Perhaps I don't always stray far, but little choices – neglecting my scripture reading to watch TV, skipping a prayer before a meal or not offering help to someone in need – lead me away from God.

Although paths leading away from our spiritual home may seem tempting, Christ's death and resurrection promise us a greater reward in God's house for eternity. When we are tempted to leave the safety and security of God's home, we can always turn to him for direction through prayer and meditation. If we do go astray, he is always waiting for us to return. The joy and celebration when the lost return to God's home are unfathomable (see Luke 15:7, 10). God's arms are always open and waiting for the lost to return.

Prayer: *Dear God, thank you for your abundant grace. If we lose our way, help us to find the path back to your love and forgiveness. Amen*

Thought for the day: I can always turn to God for safety and direction.

Chad Zeleny (Iowa, US)

Where the water begins

Read John 7:37–39

The Lord will guide you always; he will satisfy your needs in a sun-scorched land and will strengthen your frame. You will be like a well-watered garden, like a spring whose waters never fail.
Isaiah 58:11 (NIV)

I love to sit and watch the stream that flows at the bottom of our garden. Sometimes, during dry spells, it slows; but it keeps moving. Streams and rivers flow continually all around the area where I live. I've often sat beside a fast-moving mountain stream and wondered, 'Where is all that water coming from? What keeps the water flowing? Where does it begin?'

When I watch the water rippling in the stream, I honestly don't know where it begins. However, I do know the source for the spiritual water in my life. Isaiah says that God will make us to be like springs whose waters never fail. He promises to satisfy our needs and to strengthen us, to send us blessings and to work in us. God's grace and love continue to flow through me – just like endlessly moving water, rolling over rocks and cascading down waterfalls.

Prayer: *Source of life, thank you for your love and strength that never fails. Flow through us as we seek to love and serve others. Amen*

Thought for the day: God's love is a stream that never runs dry.

Trina Stamey (North Carolina, US)

Sight versus insight

Read James 1:2–5

Encourage one another and build each other up.
1 Thessalonians 5:11 (NIV)

As I stood to preach one morning, I suddenly lost the sight in my left eye. I couldn't see the faces of people in the congregation or the notes I had prepared for my sermon. Now, after two operations and weekly visits to the ophthalmologist, my vision is almost back to normal.

Reflecting on this experience, I began thinking about spiritual blindness. Because I had not been comfortable reading during the months after I had lost the sight in my eye, my devotional life suffered. I spent much less time with my Lord. I began to wonder, 'Is my faith so shallow that I could get so easily sidetracked?' However, when I was at this low ebb, God allowed me to see in a different way.

I saw kindness, caring, prayerful concern and support from so many people – especially my wife, Joan, our family and our church community. I was prayed for and encouraged by phone calls and emails. The support I received reminded me of today's reading and scripture quotation. This experience tested my faith, but God used the time to prompt me to introspection and to help me really see myself. I had thought that I was in control of my life when all along God had been in charge. During this experience and ever since, he has been training me in humility and patience.

Prayer: *Dear God, thank you for all of our many blessings. Help us to grow closer to you each day – especially in times of trial. Amen*

Thought for the day: How can I exercise my spiritual muscles today?

John Bredenkamp (KwaZulu-Natal, South Africa)

What's my message?

Read Ephesians 6:10–20

Let the message of Christ dwell among you richly.
Colossians 3:16 (NIV)

When I was visiting Athens, I came across a street fair with a live band and a variety of stalls. At one, a woman offered me a free T-shirt. As a budget backpacker, I gladly accepted. The next day, I wore the T-shirt, but as I set out to explore the city I quickly became self-conscious. I had no idea what the Greek writing scrawled across the front of my T-shirt meant. But all the locals would know. What if I was wearing a message I didn't support? Towards the end of the day, I ended up chatting with a shopkeeper and his assistant. One of them told me, 'I like your T-shirt.' I replied that I didn't know what the words on it meant.

The assistant translated the message as, 'There are a lot of adventures to be had in life. Drugs shouldn't be one of them.' Reassured that the message was one I supported, I spent the rest of the day feeling bold instead of self-conscious.

This experience made me think about how often I wear a message without realising it. Though not as obvious as writing on a T-shirt, the way I treat others, the words I say – and even my facial expressions – send messages to others. I want that message to reflect that Christ lives in me.

Prayer: *Dear Lord, help us to choose our words and actions carefully so that they will bring glory to you and lovingly spread your message to the world. In Jesus' name. Amen*

Thought for the day: What attitudes and actions do I need to 'wear' to reflect my life in Christ?

Jessica Lippe (Oregon, US)

Friends indeed

Read Job 2:11–13

Many Jews had come to comfort Martha and Mary after their brother's death.
John 11:19 (CEB)

I will never forget what five of my friends did for me when my wife died. Lisa died in her sleep on a Sunday morning in February after an 18-year battle with multiple sclerosis. Her death was sudden and unexpected. But my friends all came to help me. Phyllis and Keith sat and talked with me the night before the funeral. Glen travelled a long distance to the funeral. Bob met us at the cemetery for Lisa's graveside service and stayed with me during the meal afterwards. And then Steve later attended the memorial service for Lisa at our home church.

When we read the later chapters of the book of Job, it's easy for us to forget the beginning – how for seven days and seven nights Job's three friends came and cried with him and sat with him without speaking. Words cannot express my gratitude for my friends' presence with me during the hardest time of my life. I know why each of them was willing to be with me at different times: because words could not express what they wanted to communicate to me. In the same way, God loves us more than words can say. So he came in person to show us.

Prayer: *Loving God, thank you for the gift of one another's presence, through which you empower us to receive and to give. Amen*

Thought for the day: For whom will I be God's hands and feet today?

Michael L. Fraley (Texas, US)

Looming mountains

Read Psalm 61:1–8

I raise my eyes toward the mountains. Where will my help come from? My help comes from the Lord, the maker of heaven and earth.
Psalm 121:1–2 (CEB)

When my teacher helped us to memorise Psalm 121, I had no idea how big mountains could be. There aren't any mountains where I grew up in central Canada, and I didn't travel much until I was an adult. The psalmist's words meant more to me when I first saw the Canadian Rockies.

Standing next to bare, black rock, I could see nothing but the mountain. I raised my head but could not tell if the distant jagged peaks were the summit of the massive rock formation. I was too close to see the whole mountain.

Similarly, sometimes I am so close to a problem that I cannot see any possible solution. All I can do is cry for help. I wonder if the psalmist felt like this when he wrote, 'I raise my eyes toward the mountains. Where will my help come from? My help comes from the Lord, the maker of heaven and earth.'

When faced with a problem that seems insurmountable, I remember Psalm 121. When I look at the mountains, I realise that God, the maker of mountains, is greater than creation. No trouble I face is too big for him.

Prayer: *Creator God, help us always to trust in your strength. With your help, we can overcome any challenge. In Jesus' name, we pray. Amen*

Thought for the day: No problem is too big for God.

Pat Gerbrandt (Manitoba, Canada)

PRAYER FOCUS: THOSE FEELING OVERWHELMED

Hands and feet

Read James 2:14–17

Jesus replied, 'Foxes have dens and birds have nests, but the Son of Man has nowhere to lay his head.'
Luke 9:58 (NIV)

During our annual winter visit to California this year, the weather was unseasonably cold and rainy. There were many storms resulting in flooding and mudslides in several areas. At the church we attend when we visit each winter, we learned about 'The Warming Center', which is open from 1 January until 31 March on nights when the temperature drops below 2 degrees or there is heavy rain. Here, people who are homeless can receive a hot meal, sleep indoors and receive a packed lunch when they leave the next morning.

My husband and I, like many others, donate food and money to our local food banks and shelters, but this was an opportunity actually to be the hands and feet of Jesus. Setting up the tables, serving meals, getting to know the guests and cleaning the kitchen helped us to form relationships with people we might not have met otherwise. We are now able to greet them on the street by name and to pray for them. Jesus charged us to clothe, feed, visit and care for our brothers and sisters. As Jesus said, 'Truly I tell you, whatever you did for one of the least of these brothers and sisters of mine, you did for me' (Matthew 25:40).

Prayer: *Dear Lord, help us to meet the needs of those around us today. Remind us that everything we do for others we do for you. Amen*

Thought for the day: Whatever good I do for someone today, I do for God.

Carolyn Lee Purdy (Virginia, US)

A second chance

Read Proverbs 3:5–6

I will instruct you and teach you in the way you should go; I will counsel you with my loving eye on you.
Psalm 32:8 (NIV)

I was playing tennis with my friend John when I suddenly collapsed. My heart had stopped. John rushed for help and in a few minutes a woman arrived and began CPR. She was able to restore my heartbeat until the paramedics arrived. On the way to the hospital my heart stopped again, but the paramedics restarted my heart for a second time. The doctors decided that I needed surgery and, after hours in the operating room, surgeons implanted a pacemaker to regulate my heart. Within a few days, I was able to return home and eventually I made a complete recovery.

Since my near-death experience, I have often questioned and tried to understand why God spared me. I may never know the answer, but I now realise that God's ways are often not the same as mine.

When the unexpected happens or we face troubles or hardships we can't control, we can rely on our faith and remember that God is always here to comfort and guide us. Through trials and dangers such as these, we can grow in our faith and draw closer to him.

Prayer: *Thank you, God, for loving us. Help us not to rely on our own understanding but always to trust in you to lead us in the way we should go. Amen*

Thought for the day: I will pray daily and seek God's purpose for my life.

Joseph Carpenter (Tennessee, US)

Ever-present light

Read Psalm 36:5–9

[God's] lamp shone over my head, and by his light I walked through darkness.
Job 29:3 (NRSV)

Where I live, we have frequent power cuts, so it's usually wise to carry a torch when it's dark just in case the lights go out.

Early one morning I was going to the bathroom and forgot to take my torch with me. But I remembered that my mother saw me leave the room and knew where I was; I had nothing to worry about. I was confident she would bring me a torch if I needed one. That's what a mother does – protects her children.

Yes, there was a power cut that morning, but just as my eyes were beginning to adjust to the darkness, I saw a light. It was my mum standing right in front of me with that torch. I had absolutely nothing to worry about!

In our scripture verse, Job is recalling a time in his life when by the light of God he walked through darkness. Just as I trusted my mum to bring me a torch, I can trust God to light up any darkness in my life and to direct my path (see Proverbs 3:6).

Prayer: *Dear Lord, help us to trust you endlessly, no matter what hurt, pain or depth of darkness we may experience. Amen*

Thought for the day: Today I will trust God's light to lead me.

Uyo Jummai Ani (Kiev, Ukraine)

Making a difference

Read Matthew 5:13–16

Let your light shine before people, so they can see the good things you do and praise your Father who is in heaven.
Matthew 5:16 (CEB)

My energetic 70-year-old friend Mary Ann broke her leg and had to be wheelchair bound and then on crutches for quite a while. During that time, I saw a post on Facebook from one of the women of our church, seeking help with decorating for an elderly church member. Mary Ann's comment in response was, 'If you have something I can do sitting down, I will be glad to help.' Now that is a servant spirit. She has mastered the way to make the world a brighter place for anyone whose life she touches.

So many times we fail to see our potential because we allow our limitations to discourage us. But every day we are given opportunities to reach out to serve God, to love others and to make a difference. Whether by a phone call, a handwritten note or just a smile, we all have the means to make our world a better place.

Prayer: *Father God, help us to see beyond our limitations to the potential we all have to serve you each day. Amen*

Thought for the day: I can't do everything to serve God, but I can always do something.

Belinda Jo Mathias (Mississippi, US)

God's love

Read 1 John 4:7–12

I am convinced that neither death nor life… nor anything else in all creation, will be able to separate us from the love of God that is in Christ Jesus our Lord.
Romans 8:38–39 (NIV)

'They give you a steak dinner when you start work and sandwiches when you leave,' remarked the doctor seated next to me as we attended a farewell buffet luncheon for a colleague who was leaving for a job with a different institution. The wry remark highlighted the fickle nature of human interaction and how our value in the eyes of others and organisations can vary depending on our usefulness to them at a particular moment in time.

Fortunately, our value to God never changes. We are always beloved in God's eyes, and he is always there for us no matter what challenges or difficulties we face. He does not love us more when things are going well and we are obedient to his direction; he doesn't love us less when times are hard and we stray from his teachings. As today's reading says, 'This is how God showed his love among us: he sent his one and only Son into the world that we might live through him' (1 John 4:9).

We can be assured that we are loved by God. It doesn't matter if we are moving, changing jobs, or going through stressful times. He loves us and nothing will be able to separate us from his love.

Prayer: *Dear God, thank you for loving us unconditionally. May we show the same love to others that you show to us. In Jesus' name, we pray. Amen*

Thought for the day: Nothing can separate me from God's love.

Mark Karpinski (North Carolina, US)

Serving God

Read Luke 2:36–38

Come, my heart says, seek God's face. Lord, I do seek your face!
Psalm 27:8 (CEB)

On 16 November 2016, at Amigas del Señor Methodist Monastery, I was consecrated to be a nun for the rest of my life. Like Anna in the gospel of Luke, I have the great privilege of living in the house of God night and day. Anna's dedication to God through prayer and fasting opened her eyes and heart to recognise the Messiah when he arrived. Who would have guessed that the Saviour of the world would come as a vulnerable child? Yet Anna saw God in the infant Jesus.

I expect that the simple life of prayer I have chosen will allow me to see and know God in creation and in other people. In fact, I believe that all of us – through regular spiritual practices such as prayer, meditation, reading the Bible, worship and serving those in need – can become more open to recognising God's work in the world around us.

Prayer: *Loving God, help us, through your grace, to be open to your presence in our lives. We pray in the name of Jesus who taught us to pray, 'Our Father which art in heaven, Hallowed be thy name. Thy kingdom come. Thy will be done in earth, as it is in heaven. Give us this day our daily bread. And forgive us our debts, as we forgive our debtors. And lead us not into temptation, but deliver us from evil: For thine is the kingdom, and the power, and the glory, forever. Amen'**

Thought for the day: God is present all around us.

Sister Confianza del Señor (Honduras)

PRAYER FOCUS: THOSE SERVING IN MONASTERIES   43
*Matthew 6:9–13 (KJV)

'Follow me'

Read John 1:35–42

Jesus said to his disciples, 'All who want to come after me must… take up their cross, and follow me.'
Matthew 16:24 (CEB)

Jesus' invitation was for us to follow. But I would much rather believe than follow; it's easier. I can sit in the comfort of my study and believe all sorts of things: the virgin birth, walking on water, feeding the 5,000, the crucifixion and resurrection. No problem! It's easy to believe while I sit safely behind my desk.

But Jesus says, 'Follow me.' I don't want to follow because following requires getting up. It requires leaving – leaving comfort, perhaps family, friends, job and hobbies. Followers in the Bible left all those things behind. Following can be costly. It can hurt. Still, Jesus says to follow.

But I don't know if I'll like where he leads me. He has a reputation for mixing with a scandalous crowd: lepers, prostitutes, thieves. His crowd could hurt my reputation. Following might be dangerous. Again, Jesus says, 'Drop everything. Take up your cross. Follow me.'

So I've followed when Jesus calls me out of my comfortable place – to a developing country to install water filters, to a meal with homeless neighbours, to a career in ministry rather than medicine. And I've discovered that though the risks of acting on my faith are often high, so is the reward of living as Jesus would have us to live.

Prayer: *Dear Jesus, give us strength and courage to follow you – wherever you lead us. Amen*

Thought for the day: Am I believing in Christ or following Jesus?

Kevin Thomas (Alabama, US)

Deep calls to deep

Read Psalm 42:5–11

Deep calls to deep in the roar of your waterfalls; all your waves and breakers have swept over me.
Psalm 42:7 (NIV)

Children scream with delight as they splash in the waves on the beach near my home town. A little further out, surfboarders ride high along the breakers. It's all great fun, but it is another story for a small boat in a storm. Then the waves can kill.

I watched as two people walked across to the sea and plunged into its depths. Fitted with wet suits and diving equipment, they were intent on exploring the sea *below* the surface, looking for old shipwrecks. Down in the deep water, they were unaffected by tossing waves and storms.

Deep calls to deep – and that is the place where God is working his purposes in his children. I may be downcast and my soul 'disturbed within me', but I remember that in the depths of my soul God gives that peace which passes all understanding. In that deep place with God, I am still.

Prayer: *When my heart is troubled and overwhelmed, I turn to you, O Lord. Help me to find peace deep within my soul. Amen*

Thought for the day: My God calls me out of the shallows into his deeps.

Marion Turnbull (Liverpool, England)

Ancient light

Read John 1:1–18

The true light that gives light to everyone was coming into the world.
John 1:9 (NIV)

We spent three nights in a small, remote Cape coastal village. Due to the absence of light pollution, the night sky was ablaze with stars, planets and all manner of twinkling light. The Milky Way and the rest of the cosmos were vividly on display. As I gazed in awe at the magnificence, I was struck by the fact that the light I was seeing was ancient light. Some of the stars might already have expired, but their light was still travelling to earth due to the immense distance.

Jesus said, 'I am the light of the world.' Thousands of years later, this message is still true. His light has not expired in the lives of millions of people. Jesus lived in such a way that his light continues to shine through the passage of time.

What about us? Few of us will have the opportunity to shine such a bright light, but we all can shine a light that makes a difference. If we take the teachings of Jesus seriously and reflect the light of Christ in all the places we go and in the lives of those we encounter, we can make a difference in the world.

Prayer: *Dear God, by your Holy Spirit, we will let your light shine through us each day. Amen*

Thought for the day: No matter where I go, I will let Christ's light shine through me.

Roland Rink (Gauteng, South Africa)

Jesus paid it all

Read Ephesians 2:1–10

Because of his great love for us, God, who is rich in mercy, made us alive with Christ even when we were dead in transgressions – it is by grace you have been saved.
Ephesians 2:4–5 (NIV)

I work in an Alzheimer's unit at a care home. When I tell residents that it's lunchtime, it's not uncommon for them to tell me they have no money to pay for their meals. Sometimes, even though they may be hungry, they won't go to the table if they think that they owe the care home money. I find great joy in telling them, 'Your meal has been paid for.' Surprised, they often look at me and ask who paid for it. I tell them that a loved one did, and they seem happy and relieved. Some residents will still act as if they don't believe me when I say it's been paid for. So, once again, I reassure them that they don't owe anything.

Every time I tell them, 'Your meal has been paid for,' I think of the passage above. Many of us don't like to have an outstanding bill or to owe anyone. We strive to pay off our debts until we owe nothing. The truth is that we may owe God everything, but we can never repay him for all we have received. Certainly, we aren't worthy of Jesus' dying on the cross for us. God simply loves us that much. When I doubt my worthiness, I know that God is saying to me, 'It is by grace you have been saved.'

Prayer: *Dear God, help us to rejoice in knowing that our sins were paid for by your Son, Jesus Christ. Amen*

Thought for the day: Jesus paid the ultimate price for my sins.

Jenny McBride (Alabama, US)

Soaring

Read Isaiah 40:28–31

Those who hope in the Lord will renew their strength. They will soar on wings like eagles.
Isaiah 40:31 (NIV)

One beautiful autumn day, I took the day off to go for a hike in the mountains to an area where I knew there were many birds of prey. With binoculars at the ready, I began to scan the sky. Soon, in the distance I spied a red-tailed hawk circling slowly in a thermal. Higher and higher it soared, until it was almost out of sight. Then, turning to the south-east, it folded back its wings and began a long, rapid descent. Down and down it came, picking up speed as it passed overhead – barely above the tree tops. Finding another thermal, it repeated the cycle until it glided out of sight.

Over time, I have come to realise that with the Lord's help, I can be like that hawk. God constantly provides me with moments full of the spiritual lift that I need to get through another week. Sunday worship, time each day with *The Upper Room* or praying with my wife in the mornings are all activities that, for me, are like the thermals which enable the hawk to fly to its destination. Each day, we can claim the promise that 'those who hope in the Lord will renew their strength. They will soar on wings like eagles.'

Prayer: *Gracious Lord, when we are tired or discouraged, bring us into your presence and raise us up so that we may continue to worship and serve you. Amen*

Thought for the day: Today, I will watch for the special moments that God is giving me to soar.

Harlan M. Baxter (Minnesota, US)

'It's not fair!'

Read 1 Corinthians 13:11–13

Trust in the Lord with all your heart, and do not rely on your own insight.
Proverbs 3:5 (NRSV)

When I was eight years old, my father built a new house for us to live in. One afternoon while working on the house, he was also looking after my younger brother and sister and me. At one point, my four-year-old sister climbed up the ladder to be on the roof with my father. My brother and I also began to climb up to join them. But my father refused to allow it. Our immediate reaction was, 'It's not fair!' But Dad was adamant. We were to stay on the ground.

At the time, I didn't understand that my father was concerned for our safety. One child on the roof may not have been a problem. But allowing three bored, argumentative children on the roof together would have been courting disaster.

I am now a parent and a grandparent, and I would probably make a decision similar to my dad's. As a child, I saw the situation as my father's favouring my little sister – again! I failed to recognise my dad's sound judgement and the love that influenced his decision.

As an adult, when I think something is unfair, I may be failing to understand God's deep love for me and for those around me. Then I remember this and other similar lessons from my childhood. Gradually, I am learning to trust more deeply in the wisdom and judgement of our loving God.

Prayer: *Loving Father, help us to trust you more than our own understanding. Thank you for your love, which is at the heart of all of life. Amen*

Thought for the day: God knows best.

Meg Mangan (New South Wales, Australia)

Let the light shine

Read Matthew 6:19–21

When I sit in darkness, the Lord will be a light to me.
Micah 7:8 (NRSV)

Now that I'm retired, I look forward to my trips to a nearby country park to walk through the woods. Often as I walk, the sunlight filters through the trees and shines down on me. I sometimes find myself pausing to pray, 'Lord, where is your light in my life today?' As I continue walking, clarity often comes, and I begin to recognise those treasures that moth and rust cannot destroy.

One treasured light is the friend who is always there to listen. Other light comes from those at church who, with hearts of compassion, visit the sick and the elderly. I see God's light in my wife, as she shows love to and cares for our children and grandchildren. And God's light shines brightly in the smiles of those who thank us as they receive something to eat from the food bank where I volunteer.

Sometimes the many things with which we fill our lives can block out the light that is our true treasure. They can even keep us from seeing our Lord's goodness when it's there in front of us. When this happens, it's usually time to stop, slow down a bit and focus on seeing the Lord's presence as much as we can in all the places we pass by each day. I thank our Lord for the times I'm able to recognise the treasures God places in front of me.

Prayer: *Dear Lord, help us to see you each day in those around us. Help us to be a light to others. Amen*

Thought for the day: God can be a constant source of light in my life – often where I least expect it.

William M. Mazmanian (Michigan, US)

The little things

Read Luke 16:10–15

Whoever is faithful in a very little is faithful also in much; and whoever is dishonest in a very little is dishonest also in much.
Luke 16:10 (NRSV)

My husband and I are both bread bakers. But though we may follow the same recipes, we approach the task of baking differently. He's meticulous, checking water temperature with a thermometer and measuring flour on the scales, while I am admittedly sloppy – gauging temperature with my hand and volume by my eye. His loaves usually turn out better because these little acts of effort make a difference.

And what is true in bread baking is also true in areas of much greater consequence, like work ethic and integrity. Having integrity involves hundreds of little actions over the course of time: the choice to admit a mistake when I could easily pretend that it was someone else's fault; the willingness to stay an extra hour at work to ensure that the job I set out to do is of the utmost quality; or the decision not to check personal emails while at work.

In today's quoted verse, Jesus told his disciples that how we treat the little things is a good indicator of how we will treat the big things. My inferior bread doesn't bother me, but my style of baking calls me to examine the approach I take to other tasks in my life. What does the sum total of my actions say about the person I am and the person I am becoming?

Prayer: *O God, you see all, know all and are with us in all. Help us to make good choices in all circumstances. Amen*

Thought for the day: Am I faithful to the gospel in the small things?

Teresa Coda (Rhode Island, US)

Have faith

Read Mark 2:1–12

And the prayer offered in faith will make the sick person well; the Lord will raise them up. If they have sinned, they will be forgiven.
James 5:15 (NIV)

I serve a small church in Estonia. One Sunday morning before the service began, the phone rang and a desperate mother said to me, 'Our son Romet has been diagnosed with an incurable disease. The doctors give us no hope, and he does not have much time left. We have heard that God can help in such situations.'

'Yes,' I replied, 'God can help, and we will pray for your son.' The woman responded, 'We will come to your service this morning!' I hesitated, thinking, 'What if we fail? Can we really help this family?'

When I arrived at the church, the family was already waiting for me. We changed the order of service and took time to pray for Romet. We relied on God's promises. Some months later, the family returned. The boy's mother said, 'Romet has been healed! His doctors are amazed, and we give praise to God!'

This story reminds me of when Jesus healed the paralysed man in today's reading. Because of the faith of the man's friends, Jesus healed him and forgave his sins. Though Jesus may not heal each of us in the same way, he can do miraculous things in our lives.

Prayer: *Dear Lord, help us to trust that our faithful prayers make a difference. Amen*

Thought for the day: Prayer is powerful.

Rando Metsamaa (Estonia)

Sharing God's word

Read Ephesians 4:7–16

[Jesus said,] 'Where two or three gather in my name, there am I with them.'
Matthew 18:20 (NIV)

When I was a child, my grandma taught me to memorise Bible verses. She told me that when she couldn't sleep, she would try to recall all of the passages she had committed to memory and that doing this comforted her and helped her to be at peace. Now that I am 95 years old and spend more time at home alone, I especially appreciate that comfort and peace. The Bible can be a companion for those who are alone, but it also draws us together for worship and study.

For most of my life, I have been blessed to worship and study in communion with others. Even as I have moved to new communities frequently, I have always considered it such a blessing to be able to form lifelong friendships with the many pastors and fellow church members. I recently joined a Bible study group with women whose average age was around a third of mine. I worried I could not keep up with them, and that worry increased when I suffered a slight stroke that left me in hospital. To be honest, the group wasn't on my mind when Tuesday afternoon came around for the last Bible study class of the series. What a surprise – and a joy – it was when into my small, antiseptic hospital room walked the women of my study group, ready to share with me the week's lesson! Whether we are alone or in fellowship, the Bible is our lifelong companion.

Prayer: *Thank you, God, for guiding us to a peaceful path of fellowship with others as we study your word. Amen*

Thought for the day: I can find comfort and peace in studying the Bible.

Dolly Doss (Texas, US)

Divine adoption

Read John 14:15–21

You didn't receive a spirit of slavery to lead you back again into fear, but you received a Spirit that shows you are adopted as [God's] children. With this Spirit, we cry, 'Abba, Father.'
Romans 8:15 (CEB)

As I drove home from my mother's funeral, I was struck by the deeply sad thought that as both of my parents were dead, I had become an orphan. I was feeling sorry for myself – utterly alone and dejected.

In the depths of my despair, the Spirit reminded me that Jesus assured us that we are not orphans because he came to redeem us so that we could be adopted as children of God (see Galatians 4:5). Jesus taught us that we have a family – the family of God – that loves us, wants the best for us and is always there for us.

At times, we may feel alone and dejected, especially when our parents die. But beyond our momentary feelings, we can trust that we have a Father who will always love us and never leave us.

Prayer: *Dear Father, help us to grow into the image of your Son and our brother, Jesus Christ. Thank you for always being with us and reassuring us when we feel alone. Amen*

Thought for the day: I am loved as a member of God's family.

James R. Hayes (Tennessee, US)

Show and tell

Read 1 Thessalonians 2:1–12

Because we loved you so much, we were delighted to share with you not only the gospel of God but our lives as well.
1 Thessalonians 2:8 (NIV)

I like to invite my friends to join me at our prayer meeting, but they often refuse my invitation. One day a friend told me, 'Before you invite people to come in, you yourself must exhibit a life changed by Christ.'

Paul and his partners in Christ, Silas and Timothy, realised that people would not believe their gospel message if their own lives did not show the love of Christ.

This passage from 1 Thessalonians reminds me of the saying, 'Actions speak louder than words.' Preaching and teaching God's word are important, but we can also reflect Christ in our lives through our actions. The first believers decided to follow Christ not only because they had heard the gospel through preaching and teaching but also because of the kindness they received (see Acts 2:42–47).

None of us is perfect. But we can try to imitate the life of Jesus. Our lives and the lives of others may not change instantly; but if we continue to imitate Christ day by day, God will make us a new creation that can bless even more people. If our actions match our words, we will become more effective in inviting people to a relationship with God by following Jesus Christ.

Prayer: *Beloved God, we believe that with your love and strength, we will be changed to become more like Jesus. Help us to be salt and light for the world. Amen*

Thought for the day: How do people see Christ in me?

Linawati Santoso (East Java, Indonesia)

Through the waters

Read Psalm 46:1–5

[The Lord says,] 'When you pass through the waters, I will be with you; and when you pass through the rivers, they will not sweep over you.'
Isaiah 43:2 (NIV)

In August 2016, south Louisiana experienced major flooding, causing widespread devastation. Many homes and businesses suffered major damage and people lost virtually all their possessions. The situation was stressful and depressing.

Yet all around us we also saw reminders of God's Spirit. Friends – and even people we didn't know – brought meals. We received relief parcels from all over the country. Churches and charities provided clothing and other essentials. People came from near and far to help. A group from Los Angeles worked all day on my friend's house and gave her a new Bible. They then invited us to dinner at the church near where they were staying. These acts of kindness lifted our spirits and strengthened us.

Recovery is a long, slow process. But God worked through the actions of friends and strangers to sustain us materially and spiritually. It is hard to imagine that any of us could fully recover without the active work of God's Spirit. God brought many from far and wide to rescue us from the flood.

Prayer: *Thank you, loving God, for lifting us up when life is difficult. Amen*

Thought for the day: God always walks with me.

Glen Graham (Louisiana, US)

Faith in action

Read Romans 12:9–17

Love each other like the members of your family. Be the best at showing honour to each other.
Romans 12:10 (CEB)

At a local restaurant one evening, I saw the group of people at the next table praying before their meal. What made this so profound is what happened next. The waiter dropped a plate of food in the lap of one of the neatly dressed women; but instead of becoming angry or calling for the manager, she assured the mortified culprit that she was fine. I wondered at this for several days. This group had displayed their beliefs by praying at their dinner table. But, more importantly, the woman's compassion towards the waiter clearly demonstrated her faith. Her kindness was witnessed by dozens of customers.

Often I think about that day and how essential practising kindness and compassion is to the Christian life. However, knowing this is easier than doing it. Our jobs, children, social obligations and extended family can so fill our minds that we can forget to show these qualities. I pray that others see Christ in me just as I saw Christ in those people at the restaurant. Every day, we can allow the light of Jesus to shine through us.

Prayer: *Gracious Lord, help us to be beacons of your light each day. Amen*

Thought for the day: What can I do today to shine the light of Christ to the world?

Sheila Hester (North Carolina, US)

Symbols of victory

Read Revelation 21:1-7

The one who is victorious will… be dressed in white. I will never blot out the name of that person from the book of life.
Revelation 3:5 (NIV)

I have always read stories about Olympic athletes with enthusiasm, but the accounts of doping, accusations of unfair judges and suggestions of manipulated results have made me look for other examples of victory.

Today, I prefer to contemplate the small but significant victories that often go unnoticed. I am struck by the effort of a mother who awakens at dawn, uses precarious public transport and takes long journeys to work to support her children. I admire the effort of a person who has lived with addiction for many years to start life anew. I'm inspired by the life of a bricklayer in the hinterlands of São Paulo who had both legs amputated and was abandoned by his wife, as I learn how he has resumed his profession, remarried and found his skills highly sought after.

Whether it is in sport or in life, I enjoy stories of people who overcome challenges through dedication and courage. Perhaps that is why the author of Revelation uses some of the symbols of victory of his day – such as robes and crowns – to encourage persecuted Christians to persevere and find victory through faith. When we look to God, we too can persevere and seek victory over any obstacle.

Prayer: *Dear God, encourage us when we face challenges. Help us to persevere so that we may find victory in you. In the name of Jesus. Amen*

Thought for the day: Obstacles are an invitation to persevere in faith.

José Aparecido (Minas Gerais, Brazil)

Help is near

Read Philippians 4:4–7

Do not worry about anything, but in everything by prayer and supplication with thanksgiving let your requests be made known to God.

Philippians 4:6 (NRSV)

The phone rang loudly late one summer night. It was a carer from the nursing home where my husband was a resident. Once again, he was being taken to hospital for treatment. Suddenly, I was faced with a tough decision and felt very alone. Should I get dressed and drive the 40 minutes to the hospital? What if the treatment didn't help? My children live far away. Who could I ask to come with me so late at night?

As thoughts raced through my mind, the carer said that I should not worry, that my husband would return to the nursing home in a few hours. I did not need to come. Her words of comfort reminded me of the verse quoted above. After I hung up the phone, I asked God to be with my husband and to give me strength. My husband returned to the nursing home feeling better, and I was thankful.

Through the fear and uncertainty of this experience, I saw that God truly walks with me and that I am not alone. His loving faithfulness is always available. Through prayer, we can put our trust in him every day for strength, guidance and wisdom that can sustain us as we face the uncertainties of daily life. We only need to ask.

Prayer: *Faithful God, thank you for offering us your love and strength when we are afraid. Help us to trust you. Amen*

Thought for the day: Each day, God will give me strength for my journey.

Melinda Lazor (Connecticut, US)

Lend a hand

Read Matthew 25:31–40

The King will reply, 'Truly I tell you, whatever you did for one of the least of these brothers and sisters of mine, you did for me.'
Matthew 25:40 (NIV)

A few years ago during my summer holiday, I went on a mission trip to Roanoke, Virginia. A group from my church, along with 600 other students and teachers, served throughout the community. My group's assignment was to renovate the basement of a local free health clinic. Our job included painting the room, cleaning the floors, building and installing storage units, and painting a mural on the wall.

The work was hard, especially when the air conditioning failed. However, we made good progress and the final result of our labour made us all proud. We had transformed a dingy, dirty basement into a functioning medical storage area for the clinic – work that the care-taker would not have been able to do on his own. While we had not directly worked with the clinic's patients, we had made the jobs of the employees easier and helped them to serve the community better.

Working on that basement was one of the most spiritually reward-ing and rejuvenating experiences of my life. Because of it, I now find it easier to see how any kind of work can be a means of serving others in the way that Jesus spoke about in Matthew 25.

Prayer: *Dear God, forgive us when we put our needs above those of others, and guide us as we look for ways to serve you. Amen*

Thought for the day: With God's help, I can make a difference in some-one's life today.

Brendan Chase (North Carolina, US)

From grumbling to forgiveness

Read James 5:7–12

Do not grumble against one another.
James 5:9 (NRSV)

One night I woke up suddenly with a pounding heart and a dry throat. In a bad dream, I had been arguing with my husband over a family issue. Some time back, I had been deeply hurt by one of our family members. Over time, I thought I had forgotten the experience and had forgiven the one who had caused me such mental and emotional anguish. But it seemed that in my subconscious I was still resentful of what had happened and was harbouring a grudge – so deeply that I was continually grumbling about it to my husband.

This particular morning, through this bad dream, God spoke to me in the words from James above. As I pondered these words, I began to experience the cleansing spirit of love, which flowed into my mind and heart, bringing with it God's peace.

Prayer: *Our God and Father, we need your healing touch in our lives. Help us to remember your countless blessings so that we will do less grumbling and complaining and more loving and forgiving. Amen*

Thought for the day: God can help me to move beyond grumbling to forgiveness.

N. Vijaya Vani (Hyderabad, India)

PRAYER FOCUS: FAMILIES IN CONFLICT

The tears of Jesus

Read John 11:30–45
Jesus wept.
John 11:35 (KJV)

One Sunday when I was young, we were challenged to memorise a Bible verse. I searched through my Bible looking for the shortest verse I could find. Bingo! I found John 11:35 which contained only two words. Even I could remember this!

Now that I'm older and have stood beside the coffins of family members and loved ones, now that I have wept as they have been lowered into the grave, I think of this verse in a different light. Oh, the love Jesus had for this family! Standing at the burial tomb of Lazarus, tears running down his face, 'Jesus wept.' Oh, the love Jesus has for each of us! Even in the most trying times, even when darkness surrounds us, even when death is knocking at our door, there stands Jesus, loving us and weeping with us.

Prayer: *Dear God, thank you for your love and compassion and your constant presence with us. As Jesus taught us, we pray, 'Our Father which art in heaven, Hallowed be thy name. Thy kingdom come. Thy will be done, as in heaven, so in earth. Give us day by day our daily bread. And forgive us our sins; for we also forgive every one that is indebted to us. And lead us not into temptation; but deliver us from evil.'* Amen*

Thought for the day: When I weep, Jesus weeps with me.

Jeffrey A. Lambert (Kentucky, US)

62   **PRAYER FOCUS:** SOMEONE WHO IS GRIEVING
*Luke 11:2–4 (KJV)

All are invited

Read Galatians 3:26–29

There is no Gentile or Jew, circumcised or uncircumcised, barbarian, Scythian, slave or free, but Christ is all, and is in all.
Colossians 3:11 (NIV)

I grew up very poor, the son of a poor farm labourer. One day, I heard about an upcoming birthday party for one of the neighbourhood children that we played with. All week I was excited about going to the party and playing with the other children, eating cake and ice cream, and sharing in all the fun. But there was just one problem – I wasn't invited. I was devastated. I had never been so hurt or felt so rejected. It all had to do with social standing; my family was just too poor.

Thankfully, I never have to worry about being excluded from the body of Christ. In my church, all who love Christ, who earnestly repent of their sin and seek to live in peace with one another, are invited to the Communion table. Our Lord does not judge us according to wealth or social standing but invites everyone to be a part of his feast.

Why would we want to exclude anyone from what is offered to us through God's amazing grace? After all, we are all sinners. Following Christ's example, we can invite others into the joy of Christian community.

Prayer: *Dear Lord, help us always to be sensitive to the needs of others, and to invite them to our churches and to the Lord's table. Amen*

Thought for the day: With Christ, I am never rejected.

Gary Lee Griffin (Georgia, US)

To see God more clearly

Read 2 Corinthians 4:16–18

We live by faith, not by sight.
2 Corinthians 5:7 (NIV)

After three years of severe medical problems, my eyes seemed to have reached a point of stability. Thinking it was time to get some new glasses, I booked an appointment. During my examination, the optician told me, 'Your current prescription is correct. However, your macular degeneration has progressed over the past year.'

Sadness swept over me. My vision will never be better than it is now and new glasses won't help, I thought.

I voiced my anguish to friends who had prayed for me before. Several people shared scripture verses and encouraging thoughts with me, but the most meaningful were some lines from an ancient prayer, set to music in the musical *Godspell*: 'Day by day, oh dear Lord, three things I pray: To see thee more clearly, love thee more dearly, follow thee more nearly, day by day.' Yes! I need to fix my eyes on God – to see him more clearly, I thought. I now have these words posted above my desk at work and I think about them every day.

Of course, we don't see God with our physical eyes, but we 'see' him when we pray, read the Bible and share in fellowship with other Christians. Through these faith practices we can draw closer to God, who is always close to us.

Prayer: *Dear God, teach us to focus on you and draw closer to you each day. Amen*

Thought for the day: When I focus on God, my vision is always 20/20.

Janet Seever (Alberta, Canada)

Quiet service

Read Matthew 23:1–12

The greatest among you will be your servant.
Matthew 23:11 (NIV)

When my mum went into a nursing home, I got the chance to see the many people who both visit and care for those who live there. I remember the first time that I saw Manny. He looked tough but proved to be quite the opposite. Each day, Manny helps his mother with lunch. He gently and carefully feeds her, one tiny spoonful at a time. I believe that his patience and compassion sustain her more than anything on the lunch plate. Also, I see carers who work for little money yet show love and concern to patients who are too weak to care for themselves. Some residents cannot even acknowledge their help.

The local news sometimes features heroes who perform great service and who deserve to be recognised for it. However, many other people quietly serve those around them day after day in obscurity. They will never make the evening news. I'm sure that they would hardly consider themselves great, yet in their actions I see people serving as Christ taught us to serve. Their faithful and steadfast service truly makes them what Jesus called 'the greatest among you'.

Prayer: *Open our eyes, Lord, to those who serve with patience and grace. Help us to learn from their example so that we may humbly serve those we meet. Amen*

Thought for the day: If God is the only one to see my works, that is enough.

Andrea Woronick (Connecticut, US)

A surprise blessing

Read Matthew 11:28–30

'Take my yoke upon you and learn from me… for my yoke is easy and my burden is light.'
Matthew 11:29–30 (NIV)

I once worked at an antiques shop which also sold outdoor furniture and ornaments. The garden urns for sale were made more attractive with flowering plants. It took two full buckets to water them each day.

One morning, I noticed newly for sale an old-fashioned yoke, beautifully shaped and painted. I tried it on my shoulders and it was very comfortable. I pictured a milkmaid from two centuries ago, going to milk the cow and returning with the yoke on her shoulders, a full bucket of milk at each end of it.

That afternoon, I used the yoke to carry the buckets when I watered the urns of flowers. It was amazing: so much lighter and easier to carry.

Then I understood what Jesus meant when he said, 'My yoke is easy and my burden is light.' I wondered how many yokes he had made in the carpenter's shop, yokes that would not chafe the shoulders that carried them, that made burdens easier to bear.

Prayer: *Help me, Lord Jesus, to take upon myself the yoke that you have fashioned especially for me, knowing that you will be there to help me carry it. Amen*

Thought for the day: Jesus will always help us to carry our burdens.

Janet Wood (Kent, England)

It's that time of year

I am not one to make New Year's resolutions. I'm not op[...]
it's just that when I think of a new habit or practice I want t[...]
to do it when I think of it, whether it's January or June. Bu[...]
might be different.

On Christmas Day, after we'd opened our presents and had [...]
dinner, we all went to the living room to watch old films that my fathe[...]
had made on a VHS camcorder 30 years ago. They contained nothing particularly exciting – a panorama of our back garden, my mother
sitting in a deckchair on the patio holding my sister, my father's new
barbecue, a long segment of me in my sandbox eating the sand. Skip
ahead several scenes to my grandmother's dining room where two
of my great-grandparents, now deceased, are among those seated
around the table.

How startling it was to see them in the film and to realise how quickly
three decades can pass. A picture captures a moment in time in a single
image, but this old film had preserved it in a much more dramatic way.
It's one thing to look at photographs of family members who have died;
it's an altogether ethereal experience to see them move and hear them
speak. When it ended, I sat in my chair trying not to cry.

I have spent more Christmases than I care to admit alternating
between the excitement of the season and being on the verge of tears.
I blame my Christmas blues on the fact that the day marks time for me
in a way unlike birthdays, the New Year or any other anniversary. It cuts
me to the quick. Christmas brings out nostalgia in me that I try hard to
suppress because it leaves me feeling sad and empty.

Christmas is the one time of year that I am with all my family, and I
find myself thinking about loved ones who are no longer here and wondering who might not be here next year. Absence fills the house with
as much force as the loud chatter in the living room, the smell of food
coming from the kitchen and all the other signs of life around me. I am
more aware than ever that time is moving on and that it's moving faster
than I'd like.

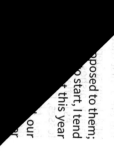

...fect that the old film had on me. It
...the truth of what James says: 'Why,
...happen tomorrow. What is your life?
...little while and then vanishes' (4:14,
...mist that appears for a little while and

...th its successes and failures, gains and
...s of pain and also the ones filled with
...d people in my community who have
...nd everyone else for whom life dealt
...l delight in the memory of a long walk
...last autumn and spending time in the
...nds. As I look back over the year, I also
look forward to the one to come and try to imagine what it might bring.

I have decided that, were I to make a resolution this year, I would resolve to let life's fleeting nature guide my motives, actions and decisions in the year to come – to be kinder, more eager to give, quicker to help, more patient with others and to spend more time with those I love. And instead of letting the rapid passing of time be an occasion for sorrow, let it be one of joy.

What difference would it make this year were I to welcome the knowledge that I am only here for a short while? Instead of leaving me hollow and empty, what if it left me more eager to love and show compassion, more willing to help when called on? What if it left me joyful – joyful in gratitude to God for every moment I am given, no matter how many or how few; joyful in love for my family; joyful in the hope of life beyond this one; joyful in faith that I haven't seen the last of my great-grandparents and all the others who have gone on?

This year, my hope for you and for me is that we find joy in all the sweet moments and the strength to endure the bitter ones. Here's to the time we've been given, to old memories and to the new ones we will make, and to getting on well in the year to come. Here's to the opportunity for a fresh start, a wiser mind and a lighter heart.

Andrew Garland Breeden
Acquisitions Editor

Each valuable part

Read 1 Corinthians 12:12–27

The members of the body that seem to be weaker are indispensable.
1 Corinthians 12:22 (NRSV)

I was carrying a heavy sack of corn along the path to our house. Because I was wearing flip-flops instead of my usual rubber work boots, I slipped on loose stones going uphill. I wasn't hurt – except for my left little toe, on which I landed. By the next day, it was completely purple and swollen. Though I could elevate my foot at times, I still had to do some walking. I discovered how much I depend on that little toe to take my weight when I walk and to help with my balance. For over two weeks, I had to place each foot carefully as I walked in order not to injure it again, and I relied much more on my other toes and right foot.

I now understand in a deeper way Paul's description of the body of Christ – that the smallest parts are necessary and that the whole body suffers when one part is in pain. If I can be so mindful of a little toe, I can certainly be more caring towards other people, especially those whom I tend to overlook.

Prayer: *Dear God, help us to support other members of the body of Christ and to look out for those who may be feeling left out. Amen*

Thought for the day: Today, I will thank God for all that my body can do.

Confianza del Señor (Colón, Honduras)

More than knowledge

Read Ephesians 3:14–19

I ask that you'll know the love of Christ that is beyond knowledge so that you will be filled entirely with the fullness of God.
Ephesians 3:19 (CEB)

When I was at theological college, I learned about God, church history, the Bible, Hebrew and Greek. Students study these subjects for three or four years to gain the knowledge that will form them and help them be effective ministers when they leave college. People who are theologically trained are supposed to be prepared when asked to preach or confronted with a difficult question.

Paul's prayer for the Ephesians flies in the face of any efforts we make to know God on our own. He prays that they may be strengthened by the Spirit, and that Christ may dwell in their hearts through faith, not by attaining a special kind of knowledge. Then, he prays that they may 'know the love of Christ that surpasses knowledge' (3:19, NRSV).

The strength of the Spirit, Christ dwelling in our hearts and the love of Christ are gifts that a minister cannot give. These gifts come only from God through faith, not by our own efforts to achieve a special level of knowledge. God freely gives his love and presence as gifts. That's something worth knowing.

Prayer: *Thank you, God, for the gift of Christ's love that surpasses knowledge. Amen*

Thought for the day: God has gifts for us that only he can give.

Adam Benson (North Carolina, US)

Struggling to forgive

Read Matthew 18:23–35

While they were stoning him, Stephen… fell on his knees and cried out, 'Lord, do not hold this sin against them.'
Acts 7:59–60 (NIV)

I spent my youth feeling angry and bitter and, when I was 30, my marriage fell apart. But in the midst of that pain, I discovered the Bible. I came to believe that through Christ my sins could be forgiven. What relief! What joy! And yet I struggled to forgive others. I read the parable of the unmerciful servant many times, but my mind still dwelled on how others had hurt me. Many of these hurts were trivial compared to sins other Christians told me that they had forgiven; nonetheless, my heart clung to bitterness.

Then one day, as I read the book of Acts, I read Stephen's prayer as he was stoned to death. He did not pray for help to forgive his attackers; he did not quantify the relative pain of stoning versus crucifixion and lecture himself to forgive as Jesus did. Instead, he named what was happening as sin, and prayed that it would not be held against the perpetrators.

Inspired by this, I started to pray that the incidents triggering my bitterness would not be held against the people involved, identifying sin but no longer trying to quantify or downplay it. I prayed that when those who had hurt me came before God, he would have forgotten any act committed against me. I imagined films of their lives in which the sections with sin against me had been erased. And as I did this, bit by bit, my bitterness receded and my heart found peace.

Prayer: *All-forgiving God, free us from guilt and bitterness so that we may rest in your grace. Amen*

Thought for the day: God's grace can wash away all sin.

Linda L. Isaacs (New York, US)

PRAYER FOCUS: SOMEONE I'M STRUGGLING TO FORGIVE

Kisses in hands

Read Joshua 1:1–9

Be strong and courageous. Do not be afraid; do not be discouraged, for the Lord your God will be with you wherever you go.
Joshua 1:9 (NIV)

When my daughter was two years old, I needed to take her to a day nursery so that I could go to work. She became extremely anxious when I had to leave her; she clung tightly to me and cried. One day, I took her hand and kissed her palm several times. Then I did the same with her other hand. 'There!' I said. 'Now you have kisses in your hands. When you feel scared, just take out some kisses and you'll know I'm with you and will come back to get you. It will give you strength.' It worked! My daughter is now 12, and the 'kisses in hands' is still a bedtime ritual.

When I experience anxiety, Joshua 1:9 is like my personal 'kisses in hands'. I repeat this verse to myself, and it reminds me that God is with me and that I can face whatever threatens me. Looking back, I realise that this verse has been true my whole life. I've encountered difficult times, but God has been with me through all of them – sustaining, comforting and strengthening me.

Prayer: *Holy Spirit, when we feel anxious or afraid, pour your comfort into our hearts to remind us of your constant presence and love for us. Amen*

Thought for the day: Scripture offers comfort when I feel anxious.

Kristen Lowe (Wisconsin, US)

Friends?

Read John 15:12–17

[The Lord said,] 'See, I have engraved you on the palms of my hands.'
Isaiah 49:16 (NIV)

While waiting with my children to see a paediatrician, I noticed a face that looked familiar. As she came closer with her two children in tow, I was pleasantly surprised that I remembered her name and that she was a classmate from my secondary-school days. However, what could have been an exciting reunion turned slightly embarrassing when I went over to say hello and she didn't recognise me or recall my name – even after I had introduced myself! I was even more perplexed by this encounter since she is a Facebook 'friend' of mine. However, it dawned on me how easily the roles could have been reversed, that I could have been the one who had forgotten her name.

This experience reminded me how grateful I am that I have a God who not only calls me friend but whose palms are inscribed with my name. I marvel that while I struggle to recall the name of a few hundred acquaintances and former colleagues, God invites all 7.6 billion people on this earth to be his close friends!

My prayer is that I will cultivate a meaningful, personal relationship with God so that I can recognise his voice and follow his will every day.

Prayer: *Dear God, thank you for loving us and calling us each by name. Amen*

Thought for the day: God is a friend who never forgets my name.

Patrick C. Kadaali (Alberta, Canada)

Ash Wednesday

Read Acts 16:22–31

I will bless the Lord at all times; his praise shall continually be in my mouth.

Psalm 34:1 (NRSV)

I sat in disbelief as I read the message. Hundreds of miles away, my mum was nearing the end of her battle with cancer. Just two weeks earlier, she had been strong and hopeful. My emotions spilled over – anger that I couldn't be near her, sorrow for what would never be and panic as I searched for something, anything, that would make her better. As I prayed, my heart cried out, 'Lord! I don't know what to do!'

We will all face circumstances outside our control, but Paul and Silas showed us a way forward. Chained in the darkness of the prison, their bodies racked with pain from the beatings they had suffered, they faced circumstances beyond their control. Yet they prayed and sang hymns to God, and their fellow prisoners listened. God heard their prayers and in response to their faith freed them from physical prison. He then freed the jailer and his family from spiritual prison.

In my moments of desperate sadness that day, I chose to praise God, swapping anger for thankfulness for his presence. Sorrow over what is lost has been replaced with praise for what I had and for the promise of eternity. Panic moved out and peace moved in. When we don't know what to do, we can do what we know how to do: offer praise and trust God to free us from the hardships that hold us captive.

Prayer: *Dear God, help us to keep your praise continually on our lips and in our hearts. Amen*

Thought for the day: When I praise God, my worries and sadness are placed in the shadow of his greatness.

Shelley Pierce (Tennessee, US)

Look forward

Read Philippians 3:10–14

*Forgetting what is behind and straining towards what is ahead,
I press on towards the goal to win the prize for which God has called
me heavenwards in Christ Jesus.*
Philippians 3:13–14 (NIV)

My husband Jim and I enjoy a well-cared-for vegetable garden. We like nothing better than fresh vegetables, and looking at those straight rows of plants gives us a sense of accomplishment.

Jim was a truck driver and away from home several days at a time. Thinking that I would help him by cultivating the radishes, I got on the tractor, started it, put it in gear and drove down the row. Jim had instructed me: 'When you cultivate, you must never look back. If you turn to look behind, you throw an "S" in the row.' Forgetting his advice, I looked over my shoulder once. That's all it took. When I got to the end of the row, I turned to survey my work. To my dismay, a large section of the radishes was upside down with the roots exposed. No amount of replanting helped. That whole section died.

As believers, we may be tempted to look back. But when we focus too much on past failures, we can forget that Jesus has forgiven our sins. Paul gives us a better way: to press forwards to the prize that awaits those who follow Jesus Christ and learn from his example. Rather than harming our future path of life by looking back, we can keep our eyes on Jesus, 'the author and finisher of our faith' (Hebrews 12:2, KJV).

Prayer: *Dear God, help us not to look back at past failures. May we keep our eyes on Jesus and walk the path that he desires for all believers. Amen*

Thought for the day: Since God has forgiven my sins, I can look forwards in hope.

Bobbie Roper (Florida, US)

PRAYER FOCUS: SOMEONE STRUGGLING WITH THE PAST

Compassionate friends

Read Psalm 18:1–6

In my distress I called to the Lord; I cried to my God for help. From his temple he heard my voice.

Psalm 18:6 (NIV)

My friend Virginia was overwhelmed and exhausted, having to go to work each day and also care for her husband, who was confined at home with terminal cancer. Tearfully, she would leave him each morning with his lunch and a drink within his reach and close the door behind her with an agonising prayer: 'Lord, how am I going to do this?'

Hearing of Virginia's dilemma, several people from our church began to help. Some provided meals. Others came to sit with her husband for a few hours each day. They would read the Bible and pray with him, chat or watch TV. Virginia told us how comforting it was to know that her husband was being loved and cared for when she could not be there.

A bit of compassion goes a long way. God had heard Virginia's distress call and prompted her community to come to her aid. It was an opportunity for us to show God's love as we followed the call of Christ, lightening her load. God was with Virginia and her husband during that time – perhaps most powerfully through compassionate friends and family.

Prayer: *Dear Father, thank you for your care, and for the hands of those who share it. In Jesus' name. Amen*

Thought for the day: God walks with me through the company of compassionate friends.

Lucinda J. Rollings (Indiana, US)

Songs in the night

Read Psalm 42:5–8

The whole earth is filled with awe at your wonders; where morning dawns, where evening fades, you call forth songs of joy.
Psalm 65:8 (NIV)

As I turn on the lights in the barn and gather the cows for their early morning milking, a few sparrows begin a soft chatter in the milking-parlour rafters. They remind me of a few choir members gathering on a Sunday morning to warm up their voices. At this early hour, I feel grumpy. I love caring for the animals, but I feel lonely. The night gloom and my mundane tasks feel heavy on my soul. My focus turns to self-pity. I long for daylight. But then I notice a stunning sparrow rhythm unfold. About two hours before dawn, the bird chatter gradually swells to a soft, slow, throat-vibrating song directed heavenward. I feel invited to join in and sometimes I add my feeble songs of praise to the bird choir. At other times, I just listen. I feel the icy heaviness in my heart melt, and joy and hope awaken in me. Yes, the darkness will end soon.

Maybe, when we become keenly aware of our loneliness or our physical or spiritual wounds, our longing for darkness to turn to light, we can learn from the rhythms of the birds' songs. Their songs reach a climax of praise during darkness to usher in the light they are expecting to come.

Prayer: *Dear God, thank you for directing your love towards us by day and causing your song to be with us by night. Amen*

Thought for the day: Even in the night, God's songs are there, calling forth joy within me.

Ron Silflow (Idaho, US)

Citizens of heaven

Read Philippians 3:17–21

Our citizenship is in heaven, and it is from there that we are expecting a Saviour, the Lord Jesus Christ.
Philippians 3:20 (NRSV)

In 2010, four of us from Nigeria were accepted to do doctoral work in Washington, DC. The paperwork was complete and all we needed were our visas. I was the last person to go for an interview. Because the other three had already received their visas, I felt confident that I would get mine as well. As the day for the interview drew near, I stood before my congregation to bid them farewell. I said goodbye to my family too because I was to leave on my flight immediately after receiving the visa. On the day of the interview I went to the embassy confidently, but I was denied the visa. I felt dejected and I could not understand why I had been denied. How could I face my congregation and family? What would I tell them?

Two years later, I applied again. Thankfully, I was given a visa and eventually earned my degree.

Today's text shows Paul's confidence in his own citizenship in heaven and assures us of ours. Paul had been entrusted with a task and he had been doing it faithfully. He awaited the day when his body would be transformed and he would enter the place of his heavenly citizenship. I thank God that we don't need to apply for a visa to get into heaven! We can live each day assured of our citizenship in heaven, with our heavenly home always in sight.

Prayer: *Dear God, help us to remember that our stay here is temporary. Thank you for the hope of an eternity with you. Amen*

Thought for the day: God's grace assures me that I will be welcomed as a citizen of heaven.

Rhoda Manzo (Gombe State, Nigeria)

In the footsteps of Jesus

Read John 14:15–19

Since we live by the Spirit, let us keep in step with the Spirit.
Galatians 5:25 (NIV)

My dad was sure-footed as a mountain goat. I never saw him stumble. As a boy, I would try to step in his steps when we walked, though it was difficult because of his long stride. If we were in the woods, down at the lake or working, I knew that I was less likely to step on a snake, twist my ankle in a hole or stumble if I walked in his steps.

I have met someone else who is even more sure-footed than my dad was. He walks on a narrow path, but his steps are always on solid, level ground. I am talking about the footsteps of Jesus, who is the way, the truth and the life. My slips and falls have been greatly reduced since I started following in his footsteps. His paths are straight and always well lit. Actually, his footsteps are clearly seen in scripture for all to follow. His invitation is to the whole world: 'Come, follow me' (Matthew 4:19).

Prayer: *Dear Jesus, thank you for making your path, the path of life, clear for all to see. As you taught us, we pray, 'Our Father in heaven, hallowed be your name, your kingdom come, your will be done, on earth as it is in heaven. Give us today our daily bread. And forgive us our debts, as we also have forgiven our debtors. And lead us not into temptation, but deliver us from the evil one.'* Amen*

Thought for the day: The more I walk the path of Jesus, the clearer the way becomes.

Paul Strickland (South Carolina, US)

A joyful noise!

Read Ephesians 5:17–20

[God] will take great delight in you… [and] will rejoice over you with singing.
Zephaniah 3:17 (NIV)

As a teenager in the 1980s, I got swept up in the punk and new-wave music craze. Even though punk was supposed to be anti-fashion, there really was a certain 'look' that we punks loved, one that was ultimately designed to shock and offend. The music and lyrics of punk and new wave were meant to do the same. I can remember my poor mum patiently enduring hours of bands like the Clash and the Ramones blasting from the stereo in my bedroom. Needless to say, she is thankful that my taste in music has evolved. I now appreciate many genres of music, including classical, jazz and even opera. Listening to composers such as Mozart or Bach now fills me with joy.

As I reflect on my lifelong love for music, I am reminded that God is a music lover too. He created it, after all. Heaven is full of music and song. Scripture tells us that the angels in heaven continually sing praises to God.

I believe God is deeply moved whenever we lift our voices in praise and adoration, making melody in our hearts (see Ephesians 5:19). And he actually rejoices over us with singing. So through any style of music we may prefer, singing praises to God is truly a 'joyful noise', for both us and him (see Psalm 100:1).

Prayer: *O God, we delight in the music we make in our hearts for you. May it fill your heart with joy. Amen*

Thought for the day: I can worship God through any type of music.

Tina Chaves (New Jersey, US)

God is calling

Read Matthew 25:31–46

The king will answer them, 'Truly I tell you, just as you did it to one of the least of these who are members of my family, you did it to me.'
Matthew 25:40 (NRSV)

I struggled for a long time with whether I should become an ordained minister. I often heard other people talk about hearing the voice of God; but though I felt a strong pull towards the ministry, I had not heard God's call.

One day, my pastor told me that the minister of a nearby church was ill and asked if I could preach there on Sunday morning. I prepared my message with great apprehension. When I arrived at the church, the people welcomed me warmly and I felt a sense of peace as I preached.

Later on, I was given an opportunity to be a lay speaker at several small churches in the area, and eventually I was asked to become the pastor of two churches. I learned much from the people at those churches and appreciated their patience and encouragement. I later started my formal training and after years of study I was ordained.

Nearly 40 years later, I can look back and see that God did call me – through the opportunities I was given and the love of people who helped me to continue even when I became discouraged.

We may not hear God's voice or see angels, but if we see a need and are able to meet it, God may be calling us to serve.

Prayer: *Dear God, thank you for the opportunity to serve you whether we feed the hungry or share your word with others. Amen*

Thought for the day: When we meet others' needs, we answer God's call.

Thad Carter (Texas, US)

PRAYER FOCUS: PEOPLE STRUGGLING WITH A CALL TO MINISTRY

A father's love

Read Matthew 7:9–12

As a father has compassion on his children, so the Lord has compassion on those who fear him.
Psalm 103:13 (NIV)

I love my father. He is an ordinary man. He did not have great wealth but he did not waver in his efforts to make sure that his children could be successful. Though our family faced financial difficulties, he told me not to worry about the cost of my education. My father worked as hard as he could to secure enough money so that I could finish my studies and graduate from university. My father's struggles on our behalf made me love him all the more. His sacrifices for our family and the love that he showed us constantly amazed me.

Even so, I know that there is a Father in heaven who loves me more than my earthly father. After all, God showed his love for us all through Jesus, his Son, who suffered and died for the sins of the whole world! By God's love through Jesus, we are saved for abundant living and eternal life. As much as I love my father, God's love goes far beyond that. His love for us cannot be measured – just experienced.

I thank God for the love of my earthly father. But my gratitude is even deeper for God's never-ending love for me.

Prayer: *Beloved Father, we thank you for earthly fathers who have shown us your love. In Jesus' name. Amen*

Thought for the day: God loves me more than I can know.

Linawati Santoso (East Java, Indonesia)

Knowing and understanding

Read Luke 24:13–31

[Jesus said,] 'Why is my language not clear to you? Because you are unable to hear what I say.'
John 8:43 (NIV)

The sermon at our Sunday service was about the two people on the road to Emmaus. They were trudging along, depressed and down-hearted after Jesus' death on the cross in Jerusalem. They had thought that his life and teaching represented a new and better world, but now all their hopes were dashed.

At this moment Jesus met them on the road, asking what they were talking about. Then he explained the scriptures to them, opening their hearts and minds to the teaching about himself. Though they already knew the scriptures, now they were starting to understand them and to grasp their full meaning. Jesus' words had an amazing effect on them: 'Were not our hearts burning within us while he talked with us on the road and opened the Scriptures to us?' (Luke 24:32).

I thought about my own reading of the Bible. How much do I really understand? Being familiar with Bible verses is not the same as really seeking out their full meaning. Now, in my devotional time, I am trying to look beyond a first reading of a Bible passage to find the truth hidden within.

Prayer: *Dear Lord Jesus, help us each day to find your truth in scripture. Amen*

Thought for the day: Today, I will seek God's message to me in scripture.

Brian Gaunt (Humberside, England)

The good old days

Read Philippians 4:10–13

This is the day that the Lord has made; let us rejoice and be glad in it.
Psalm 118:24 (NRSV)

As my wife and I anticipate the upcoming wedding of our only child, we have begun to reminisce about 'the good old days' when our daughter was a toddler, and about the fun we had as we took her to the seaside, the park or the woods to go camping. I began comparing my present life, with all its various hardships, to this idealised past. My mind began to drift into the future, imagining how enjoyable it will be when we hopefully can repeat these activities with future grandchildren.

But then I stopped myself and thought, 'What do I have to appreciate here in the present?' I began to list my many blessings. In spite of my current hardships, I realised how many gifts God has given me in the present. It hit me that someday we may be looking back on our lives today – here and now – and calling these 'the good old days'. This sheds new light on the concept of living in the moment and on not dwelling on past memories or on things yet to come.

In Philippians 4, Paul wrote that he had learned to be content, whatever his circumstances. Perhaps we too can be content by living in and appreciating each and every day, whatever our circumstances, and being thankful to God for the gift of each day.

Prayer: *Dear God, thank you for each day you give us and for your overflowing blessings. Amen*

Thought for the day: What gifts from God can I more fully appreciate today?

Scott Martin (New Jersey, US)

My loaves and fishes

Read Matthew 14:13–21

They all ate and were satisfied, and the disciples picked up twelve basketfuls of broken pieces that were left over.
Matthew 14:20 (NIV)

God has given me the gift of writing. I receive responses from readers telling me how they were blessed by the messages I've written. I am amazed at how God makes sure that the messages span different parts of the world to reach the right person in need. He uses what little I have to offer – time and the willingness to serve – and multiplies it to feed many.

We are each blessed with some gift from the Lord, but sometimes we don't have the eyes to see it. God loves a cheerful giver. It's not about how large our offering is; we only have to offer our loaves and fishes so that Jesus can satisfy a multitude. The grace and power of God help us to use our blessings to bless others and provide for all of the flock.

Whatever little we have to offer lovingly, God will take it to an altogether new level of blessing that is not possible through human efforts alone. When we share our loaves and fishes, we will see the miracles happen!

Prayer: *Giver of every good gift, we willingly offer whatever we have to you so that we can be a blessing to many. Amen*

Thought for the day: How does God want me to use my gifts today?

Deepika Emmanuel Sagar (Rajasthan, India)

Trust in God

Read Proverbs 3:5–8

Commit to the Lord whatever you do, and he will establish your plans.
Proverbs 16:3 (NIV)

When I was growing up, people always told me to trust God. I never really understood why or how. I mean, nobody can see God. So I wondered, 'What problems can God solve?' Ten-year-old me immediately thought of the biggest problem I had at the time: I would be moving soon and would never see any of my friends again.

I had no idea how I would make new friends in my new home. When I talked to my parents about my feelings, they told me to trust in God. So I made a promise to myself that I would try my best to keep an open mind and see what God had in store.

On the first day at my new school, I didn't know anyone but I sat down next to another pupil anyway. Over the course of that year, we became great friends and we're still close friends today.

Listening to my parents' encouragement helped me learn to trust God. Even now, he shows me how to take life one day at a time. Even though I didn't then understand how this advice would help, I now know that we can find comfort and peace through trusting God's plan for us.

Prayer: *Dear Lord, thank you for supporting us when life presents challenges. Help us to trust you day by day. Amen*

Thought for the day: Today, I will keep an open mind to see what God has in store for me.

Hayden Davenport (North Carolina, US)

New focus

Read Romans 5:1–5

We also glory in our sufferings, because we know that suffering produces perseverance; perseverance, character; and character, hope.

Romans 5:3–4 (NIV)

At the age of 26 and after years of study, I was newly married and beginning my career. I was young, happy and ambitious. Then, after unexplained pain and months of uncertainty, I was diagnosed with a rare medical disorder, which has become a lifelong combination of days of discomfort and remission. During the pain, I would worry that it would not go away, and when in remission, I would worry about when it would come back. Though I was brought up as a Christian, I was not actively worshipping at the time of my diagnosis, and I dealt with my condition with fear and uncertainty.

Now at the age of 45, I am a practising Christian. When I look back, I realise that this problem with my health has actually brought me joy by turning my focus to God and encouraging me to raise my two sons to have faith. I have also witnessed God's grace through the medical professionals who have provided me with relief when and where I least expected it.

This has helped me to grow in my faith, showing me the ways God provides me with the support I need to endure so that I no longer live in constant fear. In turn, my growth in faith has shifted my focus away from my own discomfort and troubles and towards helping others.

Prayer: *Dear God, in times of discomfort, help us to see opportunities to grow in our faith. Amen*

Thought for the day: God is my strength.

Andrea Weaver (New Jersey, US)

Making a difference

Read Mark 12:28–33

Do to others as you would have them do to you.
Luke 6:31 (NIV)

Two mornings a week, I take the bus into town. I find that bus ride an uplifting experience. I am constantly struck by the presence of God in the lives of the people around me. The drivers are kind and caring, often waiting for people who are running late to catch the bus. They greet everyone, not just the regulars, and go out of their way to help those with disabilities. Similarly, the kindness of the passengers is an inspiration. If anyone needs help, two or three people will immediately offer assistance – by giving up their seats to those who are frail and elderly, by lifting heavy suitcases and by helping parents with push-chairs and children.

We often think that we must do great deeds to make a significant difference in the world. However, my morning bus ride reminds me that small acts of kindness done by ordinary people are just as significant. What a lovelier place our world would be if we all treated other people as we ourselves would like to be treated. We can serve God faithfully every day by showing kindness to one another.

Prayer: *Loving God, use us to show your love through our kind actions and words to people we meet each day. Amen*

Thought for the day: I serve God when I show kindness to others.

Margaret Martin (Australian Capital Territory, Australia)

Why so afraid?

Read Genesis 33:1–11

[Jacob prayed,] 'Save me, I pray, from the hand of my brother Esau, for I am afraid he will come and attack me, and also the mothers with their children.'

Genesis 32:11 (NIV)

When I was at school, I once said something mean to a boy in my class. Mike was tough and much bigger than me, so I expected that when we went outside at lunch time, he was going to beat me up. I worried all morning. When break time came I told Mike, 'If you're going to hit me, please hit my arm so it won't hurt so much.' He laughed and said that he wasn't planning to hit me, and that he had forgotten all about it. I had worried over nothing.

Fear does serve a purpose. If not for fear, we would take foolish risks, endangering our lives. But we can't fear everything. Jacob cheated his brother Esau out of his rightful inheritance twice, and then ran away for years. When God told Jacob to return home, he feared his brother would kill him and his family. Jacob wasted years fearing his brother's vengeance – for nothing. Esau had long since forgiven his brother.

If we can do something to resolve a bad situation, then we should do it. Regardless, we can exercise our faith and turn our worries over to God.

Prayer: *Heavenly Father, we know you care about every aspect of our lives. Help us to trust you more and to worry less. Amen*

Thought for the day: Jesus tells me that worrying cannot add a single hour to my life (see Matthew 6:27).

Grant Showalter (Florida, US)

Praise God!

Read Psalm 148:1–14

All the earth bows down to you; they sing praise to you, they sing the praises of your name.
Psalm 66:4 (NIV)

In the springtime, I love to sit outside alone in the early morning chill to sip a mug of hot coffee, read and meditate on *The Upper Room* message for the day and bask in the sounds of nature. Each creature praises God in its own way.

I especially enjoy the symphony of praise performed by all the different birds that live nearby. The orchestra often includes the loud trumpet sounds of Canada geese flying overhead, the high-pitched whistles of coal tits jostling for a place at our bird feeder and a lone woodpecker holding down the percussion section in a tall oak tree.

Each bird has its own unique call, but together they generate a beautiful morning chorus of praise. Just like the birds, we each have our own distinctive, God-given voice with which we can praise him. Some people have the ability to praise God out loud for all to hear; some have the gift of quietly praising him during conversations with others; some are skilled at soundlessly praising God through prayer.

Like the birds, we can merge our unique voices and together share a magnificent melody of God's praise for all the world to hear!

Prayer: *Dear God, help us become more aware of the many reasons for praising you. Amen*

Thought for the day: How will I praise God today?

Jill Allen Maisch (Maryland, US)

God heard me

Read Philippians 4:4–9

Paul and Silas were praying and singing hymns to God… At once all the prison doors flew open, and everyone's chains came loose.
Acts 16:25–26 (NIV)

Twenty years ago, I had my first real encounter with God. I was ten years old and in my final year of junior school. When I took the high school entrance examination, I didn't know the answers to most of the questions. Afterwards I felt sad and discouraged, but my mother encouraged me and said it would be okay. She told me to pray, 'God, you are my father and mother. Help me in my examination.' I took the prayer seriously, saying it for many days until the results of the exams were published.

My mother went to the school to check my exam results. She came home and said to me, 'You passed! God heard you!' My joy knew no bounds. At that moment, I felt like Paul and Silas who, with no hope of release from prison, turned to God in prayer. To the amazement of the jailer, the prison doors flew open and chains broke off one after another until the men who were bound became free.

After this childhood experience, I imagined God as a big creature who hears all prayers. That picture has stayed with me over the years and, whenever I shut my eyes to pray, a confidence builds up that God hears me.

Prayer: *Dear Lord, help us to know that you hear us when we call. Amen*

Thought for the day: God hears me when I call.

Nwakuche Emeka (Lagos, Nigeria)

PRAYER FOCUS: THOSE WAITING FOR EXAM RESULTS

Set free!

Read Romans 6:3–11

We were therefore buried with him through baptism into death in order that, just as Christ was raised from the dead through the glory of the Father, we too may live a new life.

Romans 6:4 (NIV)

My mum was the only child born to a 13-year-old single mother in the 1930s. She grew up poor and feeling unloved. My mum was an angry woman who didn't appear to like being a mother herself. She brought us up in the same way she'd been raised, with a harsh tone and little affection. So we grew up feeling unloved too.

At school, mired in shame and guilt of my own, I began to lash out at others. The girls who seemed to come from loving and caring families became the ones I targeted in the playground. I hated those girls. My actions didn't make me feel better, though. In fact, I felt worse.

One summer during a holiday Bible club, I learned about Jesus. I learned that he loved me to the point of death on the cross and that he died so that I would not have to feel shame and worthlessness. I couldn't imagine someone loving me like that. I finally felt comforted, knowing that someone loved me. I was a new creation (see 2 Corinthians 5:17). I didn't have to hate girls whose mothers took care of them. In loving others who came from better circumstances than I did, I could actually experience the love of God and become the kind of person he intended me to be.

Prayer: *Dear Lord, give us the desire to show others love as you have loved us, and the strength to treat others well regardless of our circumstances. Amen*

Thought for the day: Once I come to know the love of Christ, I can show it to others.

Sheila Qualls (Minnesota, US)

God's rest

Read 2 Corinthians 1:3–7

Come to me, all you who are weary and burdened, and I will give you rest.
Matthew 11:28 (NIV)

One day when my daughter Penelope was a toddler, we were hosting a family gathering. Penelope was playing with her cousins in a noisy room, crowded with relatives. Penelope is a quiet, serious girl, and she suddenly became overwhelmed by her surroundings. She toddled over to me, placed her head sideways on my lap and began sucking her thumb while I stroked her hair. Half a minute later, she went back to playing with renewed intensity.

I was happy that Penelope came to me for comfort and that a few easy strokes of my hand were all it took to make her feel better. That day remains one of my sweetest memories from her childhood.

When I pray to God earnestly in the midst of exhaustion, distress, weakness or powerlessness, I feel as if he is stroking my head too. Turning my troubles over to God gives me the comfort and rest I need to face my day with new resolve. I get the distinct impression that he enjoys comforting us when we ask for help, just as years ago I enjoyed comforting Penelope.

Prayer: *Thank you, Lord, for helping us during times of distress and for comforting us with your love. Amen*

Thought for the day: When I feel weak, I will turn to God for rest.

Tim Hayakawa (Hawaii, US)

Holding fast

Read Jeremiah 29:10–13

The word of God is alive and active. Sharper than any double-edged sword, it penetrates even to dividing soul and spirit, joints and marrow; it judges the thoughts and attitudes of the heart.
Hebrews 4:12 (NIV)

During a difficult time in my life, I received an insight contained in the reading above from Jeremiah: '"I know the plans I have for you," declares the Lord, "plans to prosper you and not to harm you, plans to give you hope and a future"'(v. 11). I was unemployed, struggling with financial and marital problems, and experiencing great sadness and hopelessness. What sustained me throughout and kept me from total collapse was remembering this promise, which God will fulfil in his good time. And so, I determined to centre my heart and thoughts on the fruit of the Spirit – love, joy, peace, patience, generosity, faithfulness, meekness, kindness, self-control – and to continue to learn and gain spiritual maturity (see Galatians 5:22–23).

Faithful living is easy when everything is going smoothly and according to our wishes. But when we are tested and the reality is not to our liking or is unsatisfying, our circumstances may cause our faith to falter. I know there will be challenges ahead. But I also know that God will help me as I hold fast to the promise that his plan will be for my good.

Prayer: *God of hope, help us accept the challenges in our lives as part of our spiritual discernment. Speak to us, and fill our hearts and minds with your truth. Amen*

Thought for the day: God, the giver of all life, has good plans for me.

Monique Acevedo (Valle del Cauca, Colombia)

Honesty in prayer

Read Psalm 139:1–6

Before a word is on my tongue you, Lord, know it completely.
Psalm 139:4 (NIV)

When I stop to think about it, one of my favourite psalms can also feel a bit scary. In Psalm 139, David talks about how God sees everything and is everywhere. He sees us when we wake up and when we're going from here to there. And then David says this: 'Before a word is on my tongue you, Lord, know it completely.' God knows everything I'm thinking and everything I'm going to say! Isn't that a beautiful and terrifying thing?

Even though God knows all the unspoken words within us, sometimes it's hard to decide how we should talk to him when we pray. At times, I have prayed what I thought I should pray or what I thought God wanted to hear rather than what I was actually feeling and wanting to say. I would tell him that I was thankful when I was actually upset, or that I was grateful for his peace when I didn't feel any peace.

Thinking about my own prayers, I realise that I often hold back something from God because it feels like something selfish. But the Bible tells us that our Father loves to hear our requests. So I've resolved to be honest and say the words I need to say: 'Lord, I'm tired, and I feel that I'm in over my head at work.' 'Jesus, I'm restless. I'm struggling with anxiety. I need your peace.' Nothing is too big or too small to share with God.

Prayer: *Dear Lord, help us not to be afraid and to be open and honest when we talk to you, holding nothing back. Amen*

Thought for the day: Today, I will be honest with God in my prayers.

Adam Weber (South Dakota, US)

Berry picking time

Read Matthew 9:35–38

[Jesus said,] 'Go and make disciples of all nations.'
Matthew 28:19 (NIV)

Harvesting wild blackberries is not easy. They ripen in the heat of the summer in places with little shade. If you don't go out when they are ripe, you won't find any to pick. Also, you may go out one day and pick all the ripe ones, leaving behind those that are still red for another day, only to find when you return that the birds have eaten them. And then there are the thorns. It always seems that the best berries are hiding where you have to push through the thorns to get to them. But the trouble is worth it.

How like making disciples for Christ berry picking can be! It's not easy work. God does not always call at convenient times. He calls when the harvest is ready. It may be a neighbour who has had surgery or a young mother on the side of the road with a broken-down car. God places in our lives opportunities to sow love for the harvest. Are we ready to venture into the berry patch when the Lord of the harvest calls?

Prayer: *Father God, open our eyes to the needs among us. Give us courage and willingness to respond to your call. We pray the prayer Jesus taught us, 'Our Father which art in heaven, Hallowed be thy name. Thy kingdom come. Thy will be done, as in heaven, so in earth. Give us day by day our daily bread. And forgive us our sins; for we also forgive every one that is indebted to us. And lead us not into temptation; but deliver us from evil.'*Amen*

Thought for the day: 'The harvest is plentiful but the workers are few' (Matthew 9:37).

Kim Sisk (Oklahoma, US)

God's bottle of tears

Read Psalm 56:8–13

You yourself [O God] have kept track of my misery. Put my tears into your bottle.
Psalm 56:8 (CEB)

After my wife of 60 years died in October 2016, I began reading several books about how to handle grief. One story from a hospice indicated that shedding tears is a way of cleansing the body of toxic substances. Thus, our tears in times of grief are actually a natural and healthy response to the death of a beloved member of the family.

Reading the Bible, I discovered an encouraging verse, Psalm 56:8, that reflects a period when King David had fallen on hard times. He was in hiding from his enemies and wrote about his fear. He used the image of a small bottle of tears to capture the extent of his grief. But for David, this referred not just to a custom of an ancient funeral; for him it was an expression of trust in the God of Israel – who would uphold him throughout any and all of the trials of life.

On our kitchen wall, my wife had placed a plaque with these words from Paul: 'I can do all things through [Christ] who strengthens me' (Philippians 4:13, NRSV). When life seems to be more than we can handle, these words of faith can help us trust in the sustaining love of God.

Prayer: *God of comfort, surround us with the love you have revealed in our Saviour, and enable us to live as your faithful and loving servants. In Jesus' name. Amen*

Thought for the day: God knows my deepest needs.

Elmer A. Dickson (Florida, US)

Joy in God

Read Hebrews 4:13–16

[Jesus said,] 'The water I give them will become in them a spring of water welling up to eternal life.'
John 4:14 (NIV)

Curious, four-year-old Sarah peeped around the open door of the vestry where some of us sat chatting, waiting for the pre-church prayer meeting to begin. Suddenly, her face lit up with a radiant smile when she spied her unlikely best friend: a military veteran, returned from a tour abroad. When at last he turned her way, she ran to him and scrambled on to his knee. She reached into his pocket and began to play with his mobile phone. Gently, Matt retrieved his phone, and – assured that they would meet up again shortly – the girl ran off to play with her other friends.

I cannot forget the radiance that lit up Sarah's face, and my heart too, for I know that God wants me to experience such joy when I draw near. My very best Friend is always waiting to welcome me, but I am so often slow to set aside time to draw near, to come with the confidence of a child.

Yes, we may experience deep joy, even in earthly relationships, but we can be assured that if we come to God, we will know a well of living water from deep within, springing up into everlasting life.

Prayer: *Thank you, loving God, for inviting us to come to you with confidence and boldness. Amen*

Thought for the day: Drawing near to God can fill me with incomparable joy.

Pauline Lewis (South Wales, United Kingdom)

In the thicket

Read 1 Samuel 1:1–28

The Spirit God gave us does not make us timid, but gives us power, love and self-discipline.
2 Timothy 1:7 (NIV)

Recently, I had the opportunity to explore Yellowstone National Park with a small group. One evening, as we walked single-file through dense woods, one of the guides signalled for us to stop and be silent. As she was staring into the thicket, her face turned pale. Then she began to slowly back away. In that moment, I knew that something among those trees was dangerous. At first, I was consumed with fear. But almost immediately, I felt my heart lift as I sensed a holy Presence next to me. I knew that whatever was going to happen, I would not be facing it alone. This assurance made me courageous.

The story of Hannah and Samuel shows us that we can always find strength in God. It took tremendous fortitude for Hannah to keep her promise to him. Our challenge is to trust God, listen to his words and obey. In turn, obeying God brings peace to our hearts and our lives.

I will never know what was in the thicket, since the guides refused to say. However, as we were quickly leaving the deep woods of Montana, I stepped back to let the ones behind me go ahead. I was confidently able to bring up the rear because I felt the presence of God walking beside me.

Prayer: *O God, give us open hearts and minds to hear your words and trust that you know what is best for us. May we be obedient and courageous in you. Amen*

Thought for the day: 'If God is for us, who can be against us?' (Romans 8:31).

Leasa Hodges (North Carolina, US)

You never know

Read Colossians 3:1–14

As God's chosen people, holy and dearly loved, clothe yourselves with compassion, kindness, humility, gentleness and patience.
Colossians 3:12 (NIV)

The day after my father died, I took my 86-year-old mother to buy groceries. The supermarket was very crowded with people in a hurry. On our way to the checkout, a friend of my mum stopped to talk to her and offer condolences. I noticed that a woman behind us was frantic and frustrated because she could not get her shopping trolley down the aisle. I stepped aside to ease the flow of traffic and to allow my mum and her friend to talk to one another. The other shopper sighed and rolled her eyes as she hurried past.

Mum and her friend didn't realise that they were holding up the other shopper, and the irritated woman had no idea that my mum's husband had just passed away. I saw a lesson in that moment. During times when I am hurried, I behave much like that frustrated shopper. We never know what other people are going through in their lives, but showing kindness in every circumstance is a way to reflect Christ to them.

Prayer: *Dear Father, remind us to be patient, kind and loving towards others as you are patient with us. Amen*

Thought for the day: Everywhere I go, God gives me opportunities to show compassion and kindness.

Scott Jaskier (New York, US)

Response required

Read John 5:1–9

Jesus said to him, 'Get up! Pick up your mat and walk.' At once the man was cured; he picked up his mat and walked.
John 5:8–9 (NIV)

When I was baptised at the age of 38, I thought I would change immediately and drastically as a result of my choice to become a Christian: I would always be patient with my children; I would happily be generous with my time and material goods; I would show kindness to everyone at all times.

But time passed, and I felt like the same person I had always been. I realised that change was not going to occur without effort on my part. My encounter with Jesus required a response from me. Yes, I was given a new life at baptism, but I was going to have to live it out. If I expected to develop the virtues of patience, generosity and kindness, I was going to have to practise them – even when I didn't feel like it.

The man at the pool of Bethesda had been ill for 38 years before meeting Jesus. John's gospel tells us that, after his encounter with Jesus, 'at once the man was cured'. But along with the healing, Jesus commanded him to get up, pick up his mat and walk. Rather than continuing to lie by the pool, the man embraced the new life he had been given, picked up his mat and walked. Jesus asks us to do the same, trusting that he is with us every step of the way.

Prayer: *Giver of life, grant us the courage to embrace the new life you offer and live according to your calling. Amen*

Thought for the day: Jesus offers me new life, and then I must live it.

Jennifer Haught (Indiana, US)

The tiny green shoot

Read 1 Samuel 16:1–13

Do not judge, or you too will be judged.
Matthew 7:1 (NIV)

While gardening one day, I found a plant that seemed to have died. I was about to dig it out when I noticed its one tiny green shoot. Perhaps I should leave it, I reasoned, take better care of it and give it one more chance. I did, and over the year the plant slowly began to flourish. It is now a lovely bush that I expect to flower next spring. I'm glad I didn't dismiss this plant's potential to grow and to thrive.

When I look at people, I can so easily miss the potential within them. Thankfully, our loving God looks at our hearts and sees all that we can do. With God's encouragement and the love and care of others, we can become all that we have been created to be.

With God's help and guidance, I am learning to look at others differently. Instead of viewing them with a critical and judgemental attitude, I am trying to find the 'tiny green shoot' within each person – especially the difficult ones. I want to be someone who encourages them not only to grow but also to flourish.

Prayer: *Loving Father, open our eyes to see the potential in others. Help us to encourage rather than judge. Amen*

Thought for the day: Whom is God calling me to encourage today?

Ann Stewart (South Australia, Australia)

Birdsong

Read Matthew 6:25–34

Look at the birds of the air; they do not sow or reap or store away in barns, and yet your heavenly Father feeds them. Are you not much more valuable than they?
Matthew 6:26 (NIV)

In 2014, my son was in the hospital for an extended period. It was wintertime, and the coldness and dreariness of the season seemed magnified by our circumstance and surroundings. But at the bleak hospital, a small alcove in an open courtyard gave me great peace. Thick jasmine plants wove a canopy over an ornate bench. On either side were evergreens and camellia bushes full of colourful blooms. In the centre stood a beautiful bird table where the birds came to feed. But the greatest thing about this spot was the birdsong that echoed within the hospital walls. That small garden was full of life and nature's music.

Each day, I would push my son's wheelchair on our walks and stop in that spot. For a few moments, we could forget about our problems and just enjoy the natural beauty, watch the playful birds and listen to their beautiful songs. I often think back on that garden because it provided us a peaceful setting in a difficult season and always brought to my mind the words from today's reading. It reminded me that God cares for the birds – and even more for us.

We do not go through life's struggles alone. God's love and care go with us always – and along with those blessings, a peace that 'surpasses all understanding' (Philippians 4:7, NRSV).

Prayer: *Thank you, Lord, for your love and care. Thank you for healing, and thank you for your peace. Amen*

Thought for the day: God cares for us more than the birds of the sky.

Karen Gower Woodard (North Carolina, US)

Finishing well

Read Hebrews 12:1–3

The end of a matter is better than its beginning.
Ecclesiastes 7:8 (NIV)

The other day, I failed my first driving test. I had gone to take the test fully prepared. Two of my friends had taught me how to drive, and I had paid for extra lessons at a driving school. I had a smooth drive with the examiner, but as I was entering the car park of the test centre, I made too wide a turn and bumped the kerb. 'This mistake qualifies as an automatic failure,' my examiner told me as she showed me the examination sheet. Then she asked me to reapply for my test after 30 days.

This experience drew my mind to today's readings. If I lose sight of the finish line, I will not receive the prize. Like my trainers and friends who were expecting me to send them word of a positive outcome to my driving test, 'a cloud of witnesses' surrounds all of us. They challenge us and look forward to a positive outcome from our actions. The writer of Hebrews encourages us to learn from the faith of others by considering 'the outcome of their way of life' (Hebrews 13:7).

I have another race to finish beyond getting a driving licence. As I prepare to graduate from theological college and return to my home in Côte d'Ivoire, I want to remain focused until the end, being mindful of people whom I can help with my ministry.

Prayer: *Heavenly Father, thank you for speaking to us through life's lessons. Help us to be faithful and obedient to you every day. Amen*

Thought for the day: In the race of my Christian life, I want to finish well.

Isaac Broune (Abidjan, Côte d'Ivoire)

A healing balm

Read Romans 12:9–18

Do not neglect to show hospitality to strangers, for by doing that some have entertained angels without knowing it.
Hebrews 13:2 (NRSV)

My world was shattered when I read an anonymous letter exposing my husband's affair. Afterwards, we lived apart for a time, and I began attending a church in my new location. The church provided one-to-one counselling, and my counsellor encouraged me to join a women's Bible study. The leader invited me to a retreat and told me about a women's prayer group that prays for individuals in need. Everywhere I turned, I found welcoming, loving people. Most did not know of my situation, but their care and acceptance was a balm to my broken heart and decimated self-esteem.

Later, my husband began attending church with me. The sincere welcoming and forgiving behaviour of those who knew our situation helped him on his journey to understand what being a forgiven follower of Jesus really means.

Through it all, I realised how important it is for each of us to be warm and friendly to every person we encounter. We cannot know the pain and sorrow that others are dealing with, but in this broken world almost everyone is hurting in some way. That pain may bring someone to church for the first time. But whether they are a new or long-time attendee, each desperately needs the kindness that represents the grace and healing Christ offers.

Prayer: *O God, help me to see each person as your creation and to show each of them your love. Amen*

Thought for the day: When I offer hospitality, I may be offering God's healing.

Pamela Rosales (Oregon, US)

Daily walk with Christ

Read Proverbs 4:1–9

Be on your guard; stand firm in the faith; be courageous; be strong.
1 Corinthians 16:13 (NIV)

There have been times in my life when I have so disobeyed God and Christ's teachings that I thought I was beyond help and love. It weighed heavily on my mind that God might not want to have anything to do with me because of my sins. How glad I am that his thoughts are not the same as mine (see Isaiah 55:8). I am grateful to God that, with the help of the Holy Spirit, I am learning how to stand strong against temptation and to lean on his teachings.

Following Christ requires us to change our hearts and minds. Many things can influence our thoughts and actions and cause us to stray from our daily walk with Christ. But the Holy Spirit reminds us that Christ is our ultimate example. His earthly life, work and ministry were not deterred by anything or anyone. Quite the contrary, because of the power of his love for us, Christ overcame sin and death and offers us life everlasting.

Prayer: *Forgiving God, we count on your unfailing strength to help us overcome the stumbling blocks in our faith journey. Uphold us when we falter, and pick us up when we fall. Amen*

Thought for the day: 'I can do all this through him who gives me strength' (Philippians 4:13).

José Laguna Lemus (Atlántico, Colombia)

PRAYER FOCUS: SOMEONE WHO FEELS UNWORTHY OF GOD'S LOVE

Diligently stressed

Read Psalm 62:1–2, 5–8

Strive first for the kingdom of God and his righteousness, and all these things will be given to you as well.
Matthew 6:33 (NRSV)

I am currently preparing for auditions to become a student at a school for the arts. On top of preparing for those auditions, I have to remain diligent in my college studies. Over the past few months I have developed anxiety, and I am very stressed most of the time.

For some reason, I have no problem performing in front of a large audience, but I'm anxious about being judged by four people who will determine my future. The thought of being rejected from something I have worked so hard for brings me to tears.

On a normal day, I barely have time to take a breather and think about God. When I do, though, I can feel divine peace and love conquering my stress and anxiety. I have found that a good time for me to talk to God is when I'm driving to college in the morning. I turn off the radio so I have complete silence and thank him for all of my blessings. I don't think about what I still have to do; I just think about how he is going to take care of me.

God knows what we need and will guide us towards our goals. When we seek first the kingdom, he will take care of us as we face our problems.

Prayer: *Dear Lord, thank you for your everlasting love. Help us to stay faithful during stressful times. Help us to follow your loving guidance. Amen*

Thought for the day: I will take time to seek first the kingdom of God today.

Angelina Bassi (North Carolina, US)

Growing older

Read Psalm 92:5–15

In old age [the righteous] still produce fruit; they are always green and full of sap.
Psalm 92:14 (NRSV)

I am growing older. It shows in my face and I feel it in my bones. My body does not perform the way it did when I was younger; my reflexes are slower and I have more aches and pains. But as I grow older, I realise I am also gaining new insights and a new kind of strength.

The Bible says that grey hair is a crown of glory (Proverbs 16:31). I am still able to do the work of the Lord. I actually have more time to read and meditate on scripture, pray and listen to God's voice than I did when I was younger. Even though my hearing is not what it used to be, I am growing more in tune with God's voice. My mind is not as sharp, but I am growing more grateful for the Lord's blessings. My reactions are slower, but I am quicker to depend on God. My eyesight might not be perfect, but I am able to see God's greatness more than ever. I am learning that with age comes spiritual maturity.

In all times of life, we can be mindful of God's blessings. Every season of our life has a purpose. God does not cast us off in our old age just because our strength is failing; he can use all people for the work of the kingdom.

Prayer: *Dear Lord, thank you for using us for the work of your kingdom in all stages of life. Help us to remember that we can serve you regardless of our age. Amen*

Thought for the day: As I grow older, I discover new ways to serve God.

Jenny Calvert (Texas, US)

Grace

Read Romans 8:1–11

If we confess our sins, [God] is faithful and just and will forgive us our sins and purify us from all unrighteousness.
1 John 1:9 (NIV)

From a wheelchair, I leaned forwards beside the hospital bed of my four-month-old son, Ben, and touched his small hand. I wished I could reach his cheek below the white bandage wrapped around his head. Machines attached to tubes in his head and chest were keeping him alive. My heart was heavy – not only because we were both in physical pain from a serious car accident, but because I was filled with relentless guilt. I had turned to tend to Ben, which had caused me to drive off the road and flatten a lamp post. Now my baby had injuries to his eye, arm and leg.

Over and over, I asked God to forgive me – until I felt a whisper in my heart: 'Do not ask for forgiveness a thousand times. Repent once, and then thank me 999 times for your forgiveness through my Son, Jesus Christ.'

We rejoiced when Ben and I recovered physically but, with a gradual understanding of God's unconditional forgiveness, another quiet miracle unfolded: I came to forgive myself for harming my son. Our heavenly Father loves us so much that we don't have to come to God like beggars. Instead, we can confidently thank God for forgiving us so that we can also forgive ourselves.

Prayer: *Thank you, Holy Redeemer, for your grace that flows freely to all of us. Amen*

Thought for the day: My guilt is no match for God's grace.

Lynn Hare (Oregon, US)

Loving God's word

Read Nehemiah 8:1–10, 18

Your word is a lamp for my feet, a light on my path.
Psalm 119:105 (NIV)

When I was a child in Brazil, it was not easy to afford a Bible, especially for my parents. My first Bible was a Christmas gift from my uncle José. He had already marked it up as he had read from it over the years. I can still see it now in my mind: black cover, red edging and the smell of time. But it was special to me because it was my first Bible. Before that I could use only my mother's.

After a few years, I got a new Bible and, still later, another one. I even worked with my friend in a Christian bookshop for a time. There, I bought a brand new study Bible. Then many years later, another friend gave me a King James Version, and I started reading that one. Later, this same friend came back from a trip to the US and gave me four Bibles in three different English versions.

I rejoice that today in my country it is much easier to gain access to a Bible, and we have many versions in our native language. As I look at my little library of Bibles, I am grateful for the ways that reading God's word has helped me to grow in grace and knowledge.

Prayer: *Our God and Father, work in us to will and to act in order to fulfil your good purposes. In Jesus' name, we pray. Amen*

Thought for the day: How can I use the Bible I have more fully?

Andre de Albuquerque Caetano (Minas Gerais, Brazil)

Bearing burdens

Read Psalm 40:1–5

Bear one another's burdens, and in this way you will fulfil the law of Christ.
Galatians 6:2 (NRSV)

Sometimes when people receive life-threatening news, they can become stuck on an endless cycle of paralysing fear. But from the time I was diagnosed with stage-four breast cancer, I have been surrounded by prayers and encouragement from multitudes of people. As a result, time and again as this journey continues, I marvel at how small a burden the weight of my circumstances seems.

When the cancer moved into my brain and I was faced with brain surgery, I was reminded of a college backpacking trip in the Rocky Mountains. I had fainted and needed to descend the mountain at a much slower pace than the rest of the group. When I reached base camp, I realised that I had been carrying only the frame of my pack. My fellow hikers had distributed the other 13 to 18 kilograms among themselves.

It is a mystery, but somehow the Holy Spirit lightens the weight of our burdens through others' prayers, acts of kindness and words of encouragement. When we know that someone is going through a difficult time, a simple text, card or meal may be enough for us to relieve a portion of the burden.

Prayer: *Dear Lord, thank you for those who have helped to carry our burdens. Help us to share the burdens of others. Amen*

Thought for the day: Whose burden is God calling me to help relieve today?

Mary Wisner (Michigan, US)

'A child shall lead them'

Read Mark 10:13–16

[Jesus said,] 'Truly I tell you, anyone who will not receive the kingdom of God like a little child will never enter it.'
Mark 10:15 (NIV)

Because of illness, I haven't been able to attend church services regularly. However, I did get a surprise and blessing when children from my church knocked on my door one evening to give me a stone they had painted with: 'We (heart symbol) you!' Their craftwork now sits on my bedside cabinet so that as each new day begins and ends, their loving gift reminds me of God's love.

At times in the Bible, it seems that Jesus was truly frustrated with the adults who asked so much of him. In today's reading, he rebuked those who would attempt to separate him from children. In fact, he stood a child before these adults to give a living example of what the kingdom of God is like: innocent, open, unpretentious, unreservedly loving.

It is a sacred responsibility to raise the children in our lives to know the ways of God through teaching and example. Like a family, we as a church take special care of the children among us, through Sunday school, a youth club, holiday Bible groups and a children's choir. But there is a danger that we adults see these opportunities as only one-way. Perhaps each of us should consider the children around us and ask: 'What can they teach me?'

Prayer: *Loving God, may we be reborn with the wonder and joy of seeing you with childlike faith. Amen*

Thought for the day: Children are the best teachers when it comes to God's kingdom.

Brock Knoll (Iowa, US)

Palm Sunday

Read Psalm 30:1–12

Do not fear, for I am with you; do not be dismayed, for I am your God.
Isaiah 41:10 (NIV)

Recently, I encountered a road sign: 'Rough Road, Next 3 Miles.' Immediately, my car began to shake and bump. 'I'm glad I know it's only three miles,' I thought, 'or I might turn around and go back.' Usually in life, we don't know the duration of a 'rough patch'. Often our struggles can seem endless. Those who are unemployed, chronically ill or living in war-torn areas do not know when they will find relief. But in times of uncertainty, we can trust God's sovereignty and love for us.

When I was a teenager, my mother was diagnosed with an inoperable brain tumour and given only months to live. One morning, facing another uncertain day, I prayed, 'Lord, I can handle anything as long as I know when it will happen.' Then I noticed the poster on my wall that pictured a young woman looking out a rain-covered window thinking, 'I'm afraid of tomorrow.' Below it was the outline of a hill with a cross, and the words, 'Don't worry. I've been there before.' I felt God's peace as I realised that no matter how long the road ahead of us is or what the outcome will be, Jesus not only knows every trial we will face but has already walked that rough road before us and will see us through.

Prayer: *Dear Father, help us to know that even in the times of greatest uncertainty, we can be assured of your faithfulness. Amen*

Thought for the day: Christ said, 'I am with you always' (Matthew 28:20).

Lisa Stackpole (Wisconsin, US)

Called

Read Matthew 22:1–14

Many are invited, but few are chosen.
Matthew 22:14 (NIV)

In 1979, I was a relatively young and inexperienced primary school teacher with a vague knowledge of Christ gleaned from Sunday school in childhood. Then, in a Scottish teaching journal, I saw advertised the post of sole teacher/missionary for the very remote Shetland island of Foula. Being quite adventurous by nature, I applied for the job – and got it – without giving too much thought to what the missionary role might require.

At the time, Foula had a population of about 40 people with only nine children attending the tiny school. I was expected to lead worship on the island and conduct funerals. So I started reading the scriptures as well as religious commentaries. In doing so I grew spiritually. I have not just come to know and love God but have become empowered to share that love with countless others. I now have no doubt that back in '79 the Lord had already made plans for me.

Prayer: *Thank you, God, for reaching out through scripture so that we may mature and grow as your blessed children. We pray as Jesus taught us, saying, 'Our Father which art in heaven, Hallowed be thy name. Thy kingdom come, Thy will be done in earth, as it is in heaven. Give us this day our daily bread. And forgive us our debts, as we forgive our debtors. And lead us not into temptation, but deliver us from evil: For thine is the kingdom, and the power, and the glory, for ever. Amen'**

Thought for the day: I am empowered to share God's love with others.

Douglas Forrest (Shetland, United Kingdom)

What is unseen

Read Luke 10:38–42

We look not at what can be seen but at what cannot be seen; for what can be seen is temporary, but what cannot be seen is eternal.
2 Corinthians 4:18 (NRSV)

Everything was ready. We had hidden Easter eggs in the garden for each grandchild to find. I had prepared sandwiches, cakes and desserts. Pleased with how my many hours of preparation had come together, I photographed the table and posted it on social media. Immediately, comments began to appear: 'I love the cross,' 'How did you get that reflection?' What reflection? I looked again at my post. A cross-shaped reflection from the nearby window shone boldly over the table. How did I miss that?

I had been more focused on preparing than I was on the reason for the celebration. This reminded me of the story of Mary and Martha. I felt like a modern-day Martha, missing the one thing necessary in my preparations. 'How many times have I rushed around,' I wondered, 'making everything perfect for an event but not prayed for my visitors or for the time we would enjoy together? How many times have I concentrated on what was seen and missed an unseen blessing due to my hurried pace?'

All my preparations resulted in a happy day: the eggs were found, the food was eaten and then the grandchildren returned home. But the message of the cross remains eternal.

Prayer: *Dear Lord, help me in my hurried pace to see your presence. Amen*

Thought for the day: Today, I will slow down and look for God's presence around me.

Susan Kuhn Melvin (Ohio, US)

PRAYER FOCUS: THOSE PREPARING EASTER CELEBRATIONS

Church at its best

Read Mark 2:1–12

If one member suffers, all suffer together with it; if one member is honoured, all rejoice together with it.
1 Corinthians 12:26 (NRSV)

When our son was killed in a motorcycle accident, our church family surrounded us with their love. I do not know that we would have survived emotionally had it not been for our friends, who prayed with us and for us, brought us food, sent us cards, telephoned and visited us.

In my grief, I remembered the paralysed man whose friends lowered him through the roof so that Jesus could heal him. I felt much like that man must have felt as my church family carried me when I felt unable even to walk. It was humbling to have others feel my pain and minister to me in my devastating loss. Their caring was the beginning of my healing process. Their love saved my life.

When the church embodies God's love by supporting those in pain, visiting the sick, feeding the hungry and caring for the needy, we truly act with the compassion of Christ. As a recipient of such love, I can testify that the church is at its best when we are caring for one another.

Prayer: *Dear God, thank you for bringing others alongside us to support us and to show us that you are with us always. Amen*

Thought for the day: When I extend my love to those who are hurting, I am doing the work of God.

Sam Wright (Florida, US)

Sacred moments

Read Luke 22:14–20

As they travelled along the road, they came to some water and the eunuch said, 'Look, here is water. What can stand in the way of my being baptised?'
Acts 8:36 (NIV)

Every now and again as I walk down the country road towards home after church, a sight I love to see comes into view. Lined on both sides of the road, just before the bridge over the river, is a multitude of cars and trucks. I know instantly that there will be a gathering of people on the river bank to celebrate the baptism of a sister or brother in Christ. Sometimes, I pass over the creek just in time to see that holy moment when those sacred words of covenant are spoken as the child of God is immersed in the water of the creek. It's the perfect benediction at the end of Sunday morning worship.

I can think of nothing more joyous this side of heaven than celebrating a new brother or sister in Christ. Baptism is a gift from God – a means by which we receive his grace and remember who we are and to whom we belong. We are the Father's beloved children, created by love and for love – as shown by the life, death and resurrection of Jesus.

Prayer: *Father God, thank you for giving us moments in our faith journey to respond to your love. May we never take them lightly but cherish them forever. In the name of Jesus. Amen*

Thought for the day: Baptism is a sign of God's love and saving grace.

Belinda Jo 'B.J.' Mathias (Mississippi, US)

Good Friday

Read John 11:17–27

This is indeed the will of my Father, that all who see the Son and believe in him may have eternal life; and I will raise them up on the last day.
John 6:40 (NRSV)

Avocados are one of my favourite fruits, so I decided to try to grow an avocado plant. Following the tips I found online, I stuck four toothpicks into the seed so it could rest half-submerged on the mouth of a jar filled with water – and waited.

When a month had passed with still no sign of life, I considered giving up. Perhaps no life remained in this dull brown seed. Finally, a tiny crack appeared at its base; but a few more weeks passed before a root emerged from the crack. Then another crack appeared, and a small shoot peeked out.

The seed that had appeared lifeless is now growing into a small but healthy plant. This baby tree is proof that life remained inside the seed, despite outward appearances.

As Easter approaches, I remember my avocado tree. How hopeless Jesus' followers must have felt when they saw him die on the cross and watched his lifeless body be carried away and sealed in a tomb. Yet hope was not dead! Three days later, Jesus would rise triumphant over death and the grave.

Jesus' resurrection is a far greater miracle than my avocado plant. But that plant shows me that even when the outlook seems hopeless, we can wait on God, who offers new life, new hope and new beginnings.

Prayer: *Dear God, help us to remember the hope we have in you, even when our situation seems hopeless. Amen*

Thought for the day: God gives me the hope of new beginnings.

Nelson Nwosu (Anambra, Nigeria)

Dawn will break

Read Isaiah 41:9–13

Weeping may linger for the night, but joy comes with the morning.
Psalm 30:5 (NRSV)

One night, my young son came to me. Crying, he told me that he didn't want to be alone; he wanted to stay with me. I held him, and I encouraged him by saying that God tells us not to be afraid. I reminded him of the verse over his bed from Isaiah 41:10: 'Do not fear, for I am with you.' He let me hold him and eventually fell asleep. Several times, he woke up crying and saying he wanted it to be morning. Each time, I held him and reassured him that I was with him and would not let him go. The final time he awoke, dawn was breaking. This time, I pointed out the window to show him that morning was coming. He then slept peacefully into the morning hours.

This made me think of the times when I have cried out to God in fear. For me, the night has been many things: the loss of a job, the chronic illness of a child, the loss of loved ones. Yet each time that I have cried out to God in the night, he has held me and reassured me. Through my tears, he was with me. Eventually, dawn will break – and with it comes the peace and joy that God promises.

Prayer: *Loving God, replace our fear with hope as we wait for the joy of the morning. In Jesus' name. Amen*

Thought for the day: God conquers my fears and brings hope and light to my darkness.

Diana Fleming (Georgia, US)

Easter Sunday

Read 2 Timothy 1:8–10

[The women] left the tomb quickly with fear and great joy, and ran to tell his disciples.
Matthew 28:8 (NRSV)

'Wow!' the visitor exclaimed to her companions as they entered the cathedral on Easter morning. Their sense of wonder and astonishment was palpable as they gazed around the transformed sacred space, ablaze with flowers, colour and light.

The surprise and delight of the visitors this Easter Day perhaps echo the surprise of the women who discovered the empty tomb on the first Easter Day. Expecting to see the body of the crucified Christ, they saw instead two angels who asked, 'Why do you look for the living among the dead? He is not here, but has risen' (Luke 24:5). Did Mary and her friends experience a 'wow!' moment as they hurried off to tell the disciples their astonishing news?

Easter Day is celebrated by family, friends and visitors gathering together in praise and adoration of the risen Christ. As our joyful voices ring out in praise, Jesus' words of forgiveness from the cross remind us that we, too, are forgiven. 'Wow!' We can celebrate Easter Day with heartfelt thanks to our risen Lord and Saviour, and share his love and peace with others.

Prayer: *Thank you, Jesus, for giving your life, so that we can have eternal life in and through you. Amen*

Thought for the day: I will offer thanks today for God's saving grace through Christ.

Fay Torr (South Australia, Australia)

PRAYER FOCUS: THOSE WHO DO NOT KNOW CHRIST

Caring for creation

Read Genesis 1:26–31

The earth is the Lord's and all that is in it, the world, and those who live in it.
Psalm 24:1 (NRSV)

To me, the Pacific Northwest is one of the most beautiful places in the United States. When I look at the green and varied landscapes, it's easy to see that only God could have made all this. But at the same time, we don't have to look far in any direction to see the scars that we have put on this paradise.

In such a vast area, it's easy to feel small and powerless to change anything. However, like any other home, God's creation looks better when it's clean. If I am not a good caretaker of my world, I will eventually have no world worth taking care of. After all, if I wrecked my house, where would I go to live?

In order to take care of the home that God built for me, I try to live a life focused on cleaning up our world. Recycling, using public transport and supporting environmental causes may be small steps, but they are small steps towards a solution. If my example encourages others to do the same, then small steps can become large strides. Although we may feel powerless to protect our world, if we all take small steps, the home God gave us can remain clean and beautiful, as it was designed.

Prayer: *Dear Lord, help us never to forget that we show our love for you by loving what you have given to us. Amen*

Thought for the day: How am I taking care of God's world?

Mark A. Carter (Oregon, US)

A new creation

Read Ephesians 2:1–7

If anyone is in Christ, there is a new creation: everything old has passed away; see, everything has become new!
2 Corinthians 5:17 (NRSV)

At the weekend, my husband and I enjoy watching a house-renovation TV show. I am always excited to watch the transformation of an old broken building into a functional home. Sometimes the foundations are faulty or the roof needs to be replaced, and these repairs are difficult and expensive. The best is when a forgotten beauty is revealed, such as intact hardwood floors hidden under dust and debris. In the end, a house that is an eyesore believed to be useless receives a new family.

It is a wonderful process – from abandoned to inhabited, from old to new. In a way, it looks like healing, and that prompts me to wonder, 'Doesn't God see our potential in the same way?' The Bible teaches that God is making everything new, including us. Like houses needing renovation, people are damaged. Everyone needs God's restoration. Ephesians 2 paints a powerful picture of God accomplishing total transformation in his children through Jesus' death on the cross. Our Saviour's resurrection redeems us and enables us to do good works. If that alone isn't amazing, Ephesians 2:22 proclaims, 'In him you too are being built together to become a dwelling in which God lives by his Spirit' (NIV). What a wonderful way to see ourselves and those around us!

Prayer: *Heavenly Father, thank you for the new life you give us in Christ. Amen*

Thought for the day: God can transform me from broken to new.

Katherine Briggs (Illinois, US

Make a joyful noise

Read Psalm 100:1–5

Shout for joy to the Lord, all the earth.
Psalm 100:1 (NIV)

As a young girl, our daughter, Amee, loved to sing in church. She sang with gusto, without worrying whether she was in tune or off-key. She simply praised God with all her heart and voice. Everyone in the congregation knew, without a doubt, that she loved to praise God. Years later, one of the church members commented that this sweet act of worship still resonated with her.

In the Psalms, I read how David praised God, even when he was being pursued by his enemies. Hebrews 13:15 says, 'Through Jesus… let us continually offer to God a sacrifice of praise – the fruit of lips that openly profess his name.' Colossians 3:16 also reminds us to allow the word of Christ to dwell in us and to praise God with singing and gratitude.

I wonder how often our insecurities hamper our worship. Do we sing more quietly because we worry we will sing off-key? Maybe we can learn to come before God and worship like a small child, not worrying about how we sound but simply singing praises for his mercy and love.

Prayer: *Dear God, thank you for the blessings you have given us. Help us to praise you joyfully and without hesitation. Amen*

Thought for the day: I will find a way to praise God today.

Carol Elaine Harrison (Saskatchewan, Canada)

A great banquet

Read Matthew 10:28–31

Blessed is the one who will eat at the feast in the kingdom of God.
Luke 14:15 (NIV)

My good friend Buck had just died. Only two months before, he was healthy, hale and hearty – or so we thought. Then he was diagnosed with a malignant brain tumour and was given but a short time to live. All who knew and loved him were still in a state of shock and intense grief.

His family planned to hold the funeral in his home state. Because of the distance involved, most of us would not be able to attend. Instead of having two traditional funeral services, his wife decided we would have a fellowship supper in his memory. After we had eaten, we shared thoughts and memories of Buck. Then we celebrated our life together with Holy Communion. It was a powerful and meaningful occasion, one which helped us to shine the light of faith into our profound sense of loss.

When I was asked to share some thoughts, I said that Jesus once compared God's kingdom to a great banquet, which had added meaning to his last supper with his disciples. I told them I was looking forward to being with Buck in heaven and that we would all then be able to share in Christ's great feast together.

Prayer: *Dear God, thank you for good and faithful friends, for the faith and fellowship of the church, and for the hope of eternity which we have in you. In Christ, we pray. Amen*

Thought for the day: I look forward with joy to participating in God's great feast.

Robert E. Townsend (Georgia, US)

On the bus

Read Psalm 23:1–6

[The Lord] makes me lie down in green pastures, he leads me beside quiet waters, he refreshes my soul.
Psalm 23:2–3 (NIV)

One day, I was travelling on the local bus for the disabled when an older man who could not walk well got on and made fun of me because of my height. It put a huge frown on my face. When he saw that I was upset, he said, 'I am so sorry for making fun of your height. I thought it was funny seeing such a short young lady riding on the bus.'

I replied, 'I am short because of chemo and other complications from a brain tumour I had when I was five years old.' He apologised again, and he and I smiled and talked to each other all the way to his home. Before he got off the bus, he turned and said, 'I hope that the rest of your day is good!'

When I hear mean words like that bus rider's or struggle with my disabilities, I think about Psalm 23. Its words uplift me and give me courage in difficult situations. That day, it helped me to speak to that man, and it made our journey together better. The comforting words of Psalm 23 help me to live with my disabilities.

Prayer: *Thank you, God, for creating and loving all of us. Lead us on new paths to accept people we meet who are different from us. Amen*

Thought for the day: The Bible provides words to soothe my soul.

Eve Newman (Minnesota, US)

Great in the kingdom

Read Romans 2:17–21

You… who teach others, do you not teach yourself? You who preach against stealing, do you steal? You who say that people should not commit adultery, do you commit adultery?
Romans 2:21–22 (NIV)

Some years back, I was asked to teach a Bible study class. I was reluctant to do it, and the organiser of the classes asked me why. I replied that it wasn't about the teaching but that I didn't want to be a hypocrite. If I was going to teach the word of God, I would have to watch the way I lived. If I have not been serious in my walk with the Lord, I now must begin to be. I must settle down to first teach myself, follow the word in my day-to-day life and only then teach others to do the same.

We don't become great in the kingdom of God by merely teaching the word of God but by obeying it, practising it and then teaching it. Jesus isn't delighted in a life that only teaches the word without practising it. Instead, he both taught his disciples and set a good example for them in leading a life of faithful obedience to God.

Prayer: *Dear Father, help us to follow you and act on your word daily. In Jesus' name. Amen*

Thought for the day: I can teach others about Christ through the life I lead.

Fisayo Peters (Lagos, Nigeria)

Quiet comfort

Read Job 1:13–22

[Job's friends] sat with him on the ground for seven days and seven nights, and no one spoke a word to him, for they saw that his suffering was very great.
Job 2:13 (NRSV)

As my grandfather's health began to decline, I visited him often. When my extended family heard that his health had taken a turn for the worse, they all came to see him, ensuring that he would never be alone. We sat in his hospital room in silence, day and night, praying he would get better.

During this time, I thought about Job. Even after deep loss, he remained faithful and praised God. In Job 2:13, Job's friends came to visit him. They sat beside him for seven days and nights in silence, comforting him without using words. Quiet comfort can be the best gift for a grieving or hurt person. In times where sorrow is too deep for words, the act of just being with the person speaks volumes.

The days of silence and comfort helped Job to think through and deal with his sadness, while having the support he needed. Sometimes we feel we cannot comfort someone who is experiencing great grief or sorrow because we don't know what to say, but in difficult times, silent companionship is a good way to remind others that they are loved.

Prayer: *Dear Lord, help us remember that you are always with us and that we can feel your love through the companionship of others. Amen*

Thought for the day: My presence can remind others that God loves them.

Paul Farley (North Carolina, US)

Miraculous provision

Read 2 Kings 4:1–7

Let the favour of the Lord our God be upon us, and prosper for us the work of our hands – O prosper the work of our hands!
Psalm 90:17 (NRSV)

As I am a freelance writer, my income is not always steady. When my finances tighten, it can be embarrassing to admit that I can't afford certain necessities. The last thing I want to do is make my need known to those around me, but that is exactly what Elisha instructed the indebted widow to do in today's reading. By asking her neighbours for empty vessels, then faithfully offering God the only resource she had – a small jar of oil – the widow opened an opportunity for her family and her community to witness God's hand at work. He rewarded her faith and obedience with the miraculous provision of exactly what she needed.

God encourages us to offer our resources and efforts like the widow did so that his power and loving care can be shown through them as well. Where we see deficiency, God sees an opportunity to show love and kindness to us. Trusting him with our energy and possessions is one way we can exercise our faith. What a comfort and blessing it is to know that whatever we offer, whether little or much, is made miraculous in God's hands!

Prayer: *Dear Lord, thank you for providing for us in times of need. Help us to trust you obediently with all you have given us. Amen*

Thought for the day: God provides for me in miraculous ways.

Megan L. Anderson (Indiana, US)

Stars

Read Philippians 2:14–16
You will shine among them like stars in the sky as you hold firmly to the word of life.
Philippians 2:15–16 (NIV)

A part of me has always wanted to be a star. As a child, I dreamed of joining the circus, where I would perform stunts that would amaze the audience. That dream ended abruptly, however, when I catapulted my young nephew across the living room, missing the pillow net that I had constructed. At another time, I imagined a career as an athlete. But no team out there was willing to take a chance on someone who couldn't run fast, throw far or catch a ball consistently. My teenage years were filled with ambitions of being a rock star, but the band broke up way too soon, and my musician friends and I went our separate ways. Perhaps I was never cut out for that kind of stardom.

Still, God has made each of us stars in a different sense of the word. Designed in God's image, created for his purposes, redeemed through the cross and set free to serve, we are called to shine the light of Christ in some pretty dark places. Jesus proclaimed, 'I am the light of the world' (John 9:5). He also said that we, as Christ's followers, are the light of the world (Matthew 5:14). Each of us has been given the ability to shine the light of Jesus to those around us. Collectively, the light that shines through each of us can change the world.

Prayer: *Dear God, help us to shine the light of Christ as we share the good news with others. In Jesus' name, we pray. Amen*

Thought for the day: I am called to shine the light of Jesus.

Chuck Kralik (Missouri, US)

PRAYER FOCUS: FOR OPPORTUNITIES TO SHARE THE GOSPEL

Small group questions

Wednesday 2 January

1 Have there been times when, like Julu, you have struggled to see the newness of your life? What kept you from noticing or feeling that newness?

2 What changes have you seen in your life that indicate the new life you have found in Christ? What does becoming a new creation in Christ look like?

3 What spiritual practices help you to renew your spirit? What new practice would you like to try in the coming week?

4 Are there scripture verses that help you feel rejuvenated in your spiritual life? What about these verses in particular speaks to you?

5 What rituals or practices does your church have to acknowledge or celebrate new life in Christ? Are these meaningful to you? Why or why not?

Wednesday 9 January

1 Recall a time when you 'pulled the canopy over your eyes', only to realise later that God was trying to tell you something. Why did you behave in that way? What helped you to remove the canopy and see God's blessings?

2 Who in your life helps you to recognise and celebrate God's blessings? What can you learn from this person?

3 Describe a time when you chose to be open to God and to trust his promises fully. What was your experience?

4 Name some promises God makes in scripture. Which of these promises are most comforting to you? Which are most challenging or confusing?

5 Do you find it easier to rely on yourself sometimes, rather than turn to God? Why or why not?

Wednesday 16 January

1 Have you ever dismissed others because you didn't feel you had time for them? What did you do to rectify the situation?

2 What helps you to step away from the busyness of your life in order to focus on showing Christ's love to others?

3 What does it look like to live like Jesus, walking in his footsteps? Name some specific ways you show Christ's love to others.

4 Do you find it more difficult to live like Christ when life gets busy? What scripture verses or spiritual practices help you to follow Christ's example?

5 How does your church model Christ's love to the people in your community? In what new ways could you or others in your church shine the light of Christ beyond the church walls?

Wednesday 23 January

1 Describe a time when you worried that you did not have enough – enough money, enough food, enough energy, etc. What helped you to get through that experience?

2 What does a life rich in faith look like for you? What blessings do you find in spiritual wealth?

3 Are there times when you struggle to live a life of Christian discipline? When you find yourself focusing more on earthly concerns or if you notice you are not making as much time for your faith as you would like, what do you do to refocus?

4 Do you find it difficult at times to focus on what you have rather than what you want? What are some scripture passages or practices that help you to be mindful of the blessings in your life and to give thanks?

5 How does your church talk about money and wealth? What responsibility do we have as Christians when it comes to money?

Wednesday 30 January

1 Have you ever had an experience like Pat's, where you became overwhelmed by the majesty of God's creation? Describe your experience.

2 Think of a time when you were too close to a problem you faced and found it hard to see a solution. Did you ask God for help? What happened?

3 Do you have a specific prayer to ask God for strength when you encounter challenges? What practices help you to remember God's presence and strength in difficult times?

4 Have you memorised Psalm 121, or any other scripture verses? What other scripture passage would you want to memorise so that it will come to mind in difficult moments?

5 When has your church or community faced a problem that seemed too big to be solved? How did God help you overcome that problem? What did you learn from this experience?

Wednesday 6 February

1 Have you ever felt, like Kevin, that it would be easier simply to believe rather than to follow in Jesus' footsteps? Is there a difference for you between believing and following? Give some examples to support your answer.

2 Describe a time when you pushed yourself out of your comfortable place in order to follow Jesus. Where did you go? What did you do? Did you find joy and contentment through your choice?

3 Think of a historical figure who followed Jesus in a courageous way. What do you admire about this person? Why is this example of courage inspiring to you? How would you like this inspiration to shape your life of faith?

4 Which scripture verses give you courage and strength when you decide to follow Jesus? What passages help you to discern whether you are following Jesus?

5 How does your church follow Jesus? What ministries or church groups invite you and others to put faith into action? Are there ways that this could be done more effectively?

Wednesday 13 February

1 Besides bread baking, what activities can you think of where small details make a big difference to the final product? Name some of the details that make a big difference.

2 When you find yourself neglecting or not appreciating small actions, what practices do you use to remind yourself to be faithful to the gospel in the small things as well as the big ones?

3 Who has taught you the most about appreciating and paying attention to the small actions and details of daily life? How has this person helped to shape your faith?

4 Are you intentional about considering the sum of your actions and what that sum says about you? Do you find that the level of attention you dedicate to your actions affects the way you act?

5 What choices do you make in your life that help to maintain your integrity? Do you find it easy to make those choices or is it sometimes more difficult? What scripture passages give you strength and help you to make those more difficult choices?

Wednesday 20 February

1 Share a story of victory, big or small, that has inspired you in some way. How are you encouraged by that story?

2 In what ways do you think the symbols used by the author of Revelation provided encouragement to persecuted Christians in that time? What symbols provide encouragement and hope to you during challenging times?

3 When you're met with an obstacle, how do you overcome it? What spiritual practices bring you the strength and comfort to persevere?

4 Have you met with an obstacle that made you want to give up? How did your faith allow you to persevere in spite of adversity?

5 How does your church encourage people to persevere in faithful living? How do people in your community support one another during times of struggle? How could your church be more encouraging or supportive?

Wednesday 27 February

1 Think about a time you witnessed an act of service performed quietly, with nothing given in return to the person serving. How did seeing quiet service affect you?

2 Do you ever find it frustrating that some people get praise for their actions while others often get no acknowledgement for their service? What spiritual practice reminds you that serving like Jesus often means serving without personal gain?

3 Name some ways you already serve others. Whom else would you like to be able to serve? What other ways would you like to begin using your gifts to serve your community?

4 What stories in scripture show you the importance of serving others faithfully? What passages encourage you to serve, even if God is the only one who sees your service?

5 What needs are weighing on your heart today? What are your prayers for the world? For your church? For your family and friends? For yourself?

Wednesday 6 March

1 When was the last time you had no idea what to do? What emotions did you feel? How did you deal with those feelings?

2 When you are overwhelmed or don't know what to do, to whom do you turn? What support does this person offer you?

3 Is it easy or difficult for you to pray and seek God's help when you feel lost or overwhelmed? What prayers or spiritual practices help ground you in your faith during these times?

4 In addition to Paul and Silas, what other people in the Bible show you how to move forwards when there seems to be no way out? Which of these stories is most helpful to you? Why?

5 How does your church help people praise God during challenging times? What kinds of services, ministries or practices does your community offer to support people who are in distress? Are there other ways you could imagine doing this?

Wednesday 13 March

1 Have you ever felt called by God to some particular work or ministry? If not, do you know others who have felt such a call? How did you or someone else recognise the call as coming from God? How did you or someone else respond?

2 How do you define ministry? Where does ministry take place? Who is called to ministry? Give some examples of ministry.

3 What kinds of ministry do you feel most suited for? How are you currently using your gifts and talents in ministry? What other forms of ministry would you like to explore?

4 Who has helped you to recognise your God-given talents and abilities? What did this person see in you that you did not see in yourself? In what ways did this person encourage you to use your talents?

5 How does your church help people to listen to God's call? What prayers, practices or groups help people in your community to discern God's will for their lives?

Wednesday 20 March

1 Recall a time when you were encouraged by someone you did not know well. What did you learn? What surprised you about this experience? What encouraged or uplifted you?

2 Margaret writes that she is 'constantly struck by the presence of God in the lives of the people' on her bus. In what situations are you struck by the presence of God? Who embodies God's presence for you through their actions?

3 Do you think it is necessary to do great deeds in order to make a significant difference in the world? Give an example or tell a story to support your answer.

4 What scripture passage comes to mind when you read today's meditation? How does Margaret's story give you deeper insight into this passage of scripture?

5 Where do you see kindness making a difference in your community? How can you participate in showing kindness to the people you will encounter this week?

Wednesday 27 March

1 Do you find Psalm 139 to be comforting or unsettling? Which verses are the most meaningful to you? Which verses are the most challenging? Explain.

2 How do you pray? Do you pray at a specific time of day, in a specific place, using specific words? How does the way you pray reflect your relationship with God?

3 Have you ever prayed in a certain way because you thought it was what you were supposed to say or because you thought it was what God wanted to hear? Did praying in this way make a difference in your situation?

4 What prayer practices help you to be open and honest with God? What other form of prayer would you like to explore?

5 How does your church teach people to pray? Who is invited to pray during worship? What words are used? Are prayers prepared beforehand or prayed spontaneously? What do you appreciate about your church's traditions of prayer?

Wednesday 3 April

1 Describe a time when you overlooked the potential in someone or something. What later helped you to recognise that potential? What did you do?

2 Recall a time when someone gave you one more chance, and it allowed you to flourish. What did you learn from the experience? How has it changed the way you feel about giving others second chances?

3 When is it easy for you to fall into patterns of critical or judgemental behaviour? How does your faith in God help you to break that pattern and see the potential in others?

4 What prayer practices or spiritual disciplines help you to look for God's presence in people and situations?

5 How does your church help individuals to grow and flourish? How has your church helped you to flourish? Who in your community needs help to do so? How will you help them?

Wednesday 10 April

1 Recall a time when you struggled with feelings of guilt. What was the situation? How did you deal with your feelings?

2 What do you do when you need forgiveness from another person? What is the most challenging part of asking for forgiveness? What is the most rewarding part?

3 When have you experienced God's forgiveness in your life? How does prayer help you to feel and accept forgiveness from him? When have you struggled to accept his forgiveness?

4 How does your church talk about forgiveness? When have you seen church members or others model forgiveness? What did you admire or learn from seeing that behaviour?

5 Name some scripture passages that help you to understand forgiveness. What example of forgiveness in scripture is the most beneficial for you? Why is it beneficial?

Wednesday 17 April

1 Recall a time when your faith community surrounded you with support. How did they show love and care for you during that time? What actions did you appreciate most? What actions were most surprising?

2 When people around you are suffering, how do you care for them? What acts of care and compassion come most naturally to you? What actions are more challenging? What kind of care do you think is most important for someone going through a difficult time? Why?

3 In the story of the paralysed man in Mark 2:1–12, with which character do you most identify? Which character do you hope to be more like?

4 Do you agree or disagree that 'the church is at its best when we are caring for one another'? Give examples to support your answer.

5 Fill in the blank. The church is at its best when .... Give as many answers as you wish.

Wednesday 24 April

1 Do you know someone like Amee, who sings with joy regardless of his or her abilities? What do you appreciate about this person?

2 With which person in Carol's story do you identify most? Explain. When have you been inspired and encouraged by watching another person worship God? How did this change the way you worship?

3 Is it easy or difficult for you to praise God with no reservations? What spiritual practices, places or songs help you to release your insecurities as you worship him?

4 How do you use the psalms in your personal devotional or prayer time? In addition to words of praise, name some of the other forms of worship and communication with God that are demonstrated in the Psalms. What is your favourite psalm of praise? How do you model your worship on the practices demonstrated in this psalm?

5 How do children participate in worship at your church? What have you learned from observing children during worship? What other ways might your church invite children to be present in worship?

Journal page

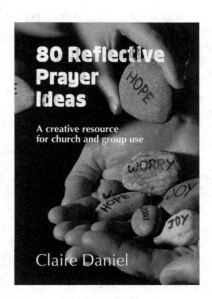

Prayer remains a vital part of Christian discipleship. Following the success of the author's *80 Creative Prayer Ideas*, this ready-to-use resource book contains 80 further ideas on setting up reflective and creative prayer stations or responses. Claire Daniel shows us how to pray with our whole being – our senses as well as our voice, our hearts as much as our minds. Tried and tested, these ideas will enhance the praying of small groups, churches and individuals.

80 Reflective Prayer Ideas
A creative resource for church and group use
Claire Daniel
978 0 85746 673 0 £12.99
brfonline.org.uk

There has never been a more important time to find meaningful and acceptable ways of passing on faith from one generation to the next. Part of this privilege and responsibility lies with grandparents who live authentic Christian lives. They can be the vital link between the gospel and the faith of a younger generation. *Faithful Grandparents* is a visionary call to an older generation to take the initiative with courage and wisdom, humour and prayer.

Faithful Grandparents
Hope and love through the generations
Anita Cleverly
978 0 85746 661 7 £9.99
brfonline.org.uk

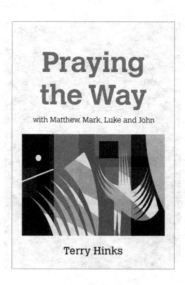

Through raw and authentic prayers, based on the gospel stories, Terry Hinks leads readers into the heart of the gospels the more clearly to see the needs and joys of today's world. This highly original book helps readers to pray out of, and with, the words of Jesus and to discover the joy of prayer as a two-way conversation – listening as much as speaking to God.

Praying the Way
With Matthew, Mark, Luke and John
Terry Hinks
978 0 85746 716 4   £10.99
brfonline.org.uk

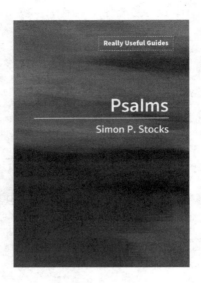

Each Really Useful Guide focuses on a specific biblical book, making it come to life for the reader, enabling them to understand the message and to apply its truth to today's circumstances. Though not a commentary, it gives valuable insight into the book's message. Though not an introduction, it summarises the important aspects of the book to aid reading and application. This Really Useful Guide to Psalms will transform understanding of the biblical text, and will help you to engage with the message in new ways today, giving confidence in the Bible and increasing faith in God.

Psalms
Really Useful Guides
Simon Stocks
978 0 85746 731 7   £6.99
brfonline.org.uk

How to encourage Bible reading in your church

BRF has been helping individuals connect with the Bible for over 90 years. We want to support churches as they seek to encourage church members into regular Bible reading.

Order a Bible reading resources pack

This pack is designed to give your church the tools to publicise our Bible reading notes. It includes:

- Sample Bible reading notes for your congregation to try.
- Publicity resources, including a poster.
- A church magazine feature about Bible reading notes.

The pack is free, but we welcome a £5 donation to cover the cost of postage. If you require a pack to be sent outside the UK or require a specific number of sample Bible reading notes, please contact us for postage costs. More information about what the current pack contains is available on our website.

How to order and find out more

- Visit **biblereadingnotes.org.uk/for-churches**.
- Telephone BRF on +44 (0)1865 319700 Mon–Fri 9.15–17.30.
- Write to us at BRF, 15 The Chambers, Vineyard, Abingdon OX14 3FE.

Keep informed about our latest initiatives

We are continuing to develop resources to help churches encourage people into regular Bible reading, wherever they are on their journey. Join our email list at **brfonline.org.uk/signup** to stay informed about the latest initiatives that your church could benefit from.

Subscriptions

The Upper Room is published in January, May and September.

Individual subscriptions

The subscription rate for orders for 4 or fewer copies includes postage and packing:

The Upper Room annual individual subscription   £17.40

Group subscriptions

Orders for 5 copies or more, sent to ONE address, are post free:
The Upper Room annual group subscription   £13.80

Please do not send payment with order for a group subscription. We will send an invoice with your first order.

Please note that the annual billing period for group subscriptions runs from 1 May to 30 April.

Copies of the notes may also be obtained from Christian bookshops.

Single copies of *The Upper Room* cost £4.60.

Prices valid until 30 April 2020.

Giant print version

The Upper Room is available in giant print for the visually impaired, from:

Torch Trust for the Blind
Torch House
Torch Way
Northampton Road
Market Harborough
LE16 9HL

Tel: +44 (0)1858 438260
torchtrust.org

THE UPPER ROOM: INDIVIDUAL/GIFT SUBSCRIPTION FORM

**All our Bible reading notes can be ordered online by visiting
biblereadingnotes.org.uk/subscriptions**

☐ I would like to take out a subscription myself (complete your name and
address details once)

☐ I would like to give a gift subscription (please provide both names and
addresses)

Title .... First name/initials .... Surname ....

Address ....

.... Postcode ....

Telephone .... Email ....

Gift subscription name ....

Gift subscription address ....

.... Postcode ....

Gift message (20 words max. or include your own gift card):

....

....

Please send *The Upper Room* beginning with the May 2019 / September
2019 / January 2020 issue (*delete as appropriate*):

Annual individual subscription ☐ £17.40   Total enclosed £ ....

Method of payment

☐ Cheque (made payable to BRF) ☐ MasterCard / Visa

Card no. ☐☐☐☐☐ ☐☐☐☐☐☐ ☐☐☐☐☐☐ ☐☐☐☐☐

Valid from ☐M☐M☐Y☐Y   Expires ☐M☐M☐Y☐Y

Security code* ☐☐☐   *Last 3 digits on the reverse of the card
ESSENTIAL IN ORDER TO PROCESS THE PAYMENT

THE UPPER ROOM GROUP SUBSCRIPTION FORM

> **All our Bible reading notes can be ordered online by visiting biblereadingnotes.org.uk/subscriptions**

❏ Please send me .... copies of *The Upper Room* May 2019 / September 2019 / January 2020 issue (*delete as appropriate*)

Title .... First name/initials .... Surname ....

Address ....

.... Postcode ....

Telephone .... Email ....

Please do not send payment with this order. We will send an invoice with your first order.

Christian bookshops: All good Christian bookshops stock BRF publications. For your nearest stockist, please contact BRF.

Telephone: The BRF office is open Mon–Fri 9.15–17.30. To place your order, telephone +44 (0)1865 319700.

Online: biblereadingnotes.org.uk/group-subscriptions

❏ Please send me a Bible reading resources pack to encourage Bible reading in my church

Please return this form with the appropriate payment to:
BRF, 15 The Chambers, Vineyard, Abingdon OX14 3FE
To read our terms and find out about cancelling your order, please visit **brfonline.org.uk/terms**.

The Bible Reading Fellowship is a Registered Charity (23328C

UR011

order

Delivery times within the UK are normally 15 working days. Prices are correct at the time of going to press but may change without prior notice.

e	Price	Qty	Total
Reflective Prayer Ideas	£12.99		
hful Grandparents	£9.99		
ing the Way	£10.99		
lly Useful Guides: Psalms	£6.99		

POSTAGE AND PACKING CHARGES			
r value	UK	Europe	Rest of world
r £7.00	£2.00	£5.00	£7.00
–£29.99	£3.00	£9.00	£15.00
0 and over	FREE	£9.00 + 15% of order value	£15.00 + 20% of order value

Total value of books	
Postage and packing	
Donation	
Total for this order	

e complete in BLOCK CAPITALS

e .... First name/initials .... Surname..

dress...

.... Postcode ....

. No. .... Telephone ....

ail..

thod of payment

❑ Cheque (made payable to BRF) ❑ MasterCard / Visa

d no. ☐☐☐☐ ☐☐☐☐ ☐☐☐☐ ☐☐☐☐

d from ☐☐ ☐☐ Expires ☐☐ ☐☐ Security code* ☐☐☐

Last 3 digits on the reverse of the card

nature* .... Date .... /............ /............

ENTIAL IN ORDER TO PROCESS YOUR ORDER

e Bible Reading Fellowship Gift Aid Declaration

giftaid it

ase treat as Gift Aid donations all qualifying gifts of money made

oday, ❑ in the past four years, ❑ and in the future **or** ❑ My donation does not qualify for Gift Aid.

n a UK taxpayer and understand that if I pay less Income Tax and/or Capital Gains Tax in the rent tax year than the amount of Gift Aid claimed on all my donations, it is my responsibility ay any difference.

ase notify BRF if you want to cancel this declaration, change your name or home address, no longer pay sufficient tax on your income and/or capital gains.

e return this form to: BRF, 15 The Chambers, Vineyard, Abingdon OX14 3FE | **enquiries@brf.org.uk** ad our terms and find out about cancelling your order, please visit **brfonline.org.uk/terms**.

The Bible Reading Fellowship (BRF) is a Registered Charity (233280)

UPPER ROOM is a unique publication which has a worldwide readership of some three million. Each daily meditation includes a Bible reading, reflection and prayer. Questions for small group study are also included for each week.

All the meditations are written by readers of *The Upper Room*, who seek to share the insights of their faith with others.

'I love the varied stories and choice of Bible passages. I look forward to my quiet time with God each day, using these notes. They also guide and widen my prayer horizon. Thank you.'

'I feel so enriched… reading people's personal experiences born from lives of faith, not simply doctrine or cold dogma.'

This edition of *The Upper Room* is published by The Bible Reading Fellowship, which works to see lives and communities transformed through its creative programmes and resources for individuals, churches and schools.

The Upper Room is also available in giant print for the visually impaired. For more information, see page 156.

UK £4.50

ISBN 9780857467676

9 780857 467676

brf.org.u